Our Perfect Storm

Naomi Thomas

ISBN 978-1-0980-9163-7 (paperback)
ISBN 978-1-0980-9165-1 (hardcover)
ISBN 978-1-0980-9164-4 (digital)

Christian Faith Publishing, Inc.
832 Park Avenue
Meadville, PA 16335
www.christianfaithpublishing.com

Printed in the United States of America

Dedication

To my wonderful husband, Chad. I have known since we were kids that we were meant to be together. I love you more today than I did yesterday and tomorrow, God willing, I will love you even more!

Contents

Preface

I know what it is like to be hopeless. I know what it is like to be lost. I know what it is like to be so exhausted with life that you contemplate giving up and committing suicide. I lived thirty-six and a half years my way, on my terms. I felt like the world owed me something. I was a lost sheep, and Jesus left the ninety-nine to rescue me.

> If a man has a hundred sheep and one of them wanders away, what will he do? Won't he leave the ninety-nine others on the hills and go out to search for the one that is lost? And if he finds it, I tell you the truth, he will rejoice over it more than the ninety-nine that didn't wander away! In the same way, it is not my heavenly Father's will that even one of these little ones should perish. (Matthew 18:12–14 NLT)

I am not a writer. I have never been good at English, grammar, punctuation, etc. I was always better at math. I took statistics once in college for the "fun of it." I am a nurse. I am a full-time caregiver to my Veteran husband Chad. We have been together since I was sixteen and a half years old. I would have never dreamed of writing a book. I did not want people to know the depressing details of our life together. Chad and I had an incredibly sad existence and marriage for ten years while dealing with untreated PTSD. Then, in 2015, Chad went to a Veterans Administration (VA) Hospital for help, and as they say, the rest is history.

When I tell you that what happened to my husband was criminal, I am not being dramatic, I am not exaggerating, and I am not making anything up. To quote the doctor who helped save Chad's leg and life, "When he came to me, he was under incorrect treatment and had an incomplete diagnosis. While this could have happened in any medical setting, in Chad's case it was the VA. There was negligence in care, especially by not having a biopsy to determine a diagnosis, not doing cultures to detect resistant infections, not addressing his numerous comorbidities that complicated his healing, not evaluating the severe side effects he had to the treatment they initiated, and not stopping this treatment when it was clearly not working.

"If Chad had continued with their plan, he may have lost his leg and would likely have serious complications of immunosuppression (infection, cancer, or death). Thankfully, they found the resources outside the VA to pursue other treatments. I am hopeful that we can get Chad back working in a few years, but left in the care plan he had with the VA, it is likely that he would have a lifelong disability. By the time Chad came to see me, he was so ill and disabled that his wife, Naomi, had to resign July 2016 to take care of Chad full time."

We followed the "proper chain of command." We asked for referrals and more testing, and we were denied. We had seven meetings with the chief medical officer (CMO) at the VA hospital (second in command of the hospital). We told them that we did not want to get anyone in trouble. We told them that we wanted to find out what was wrong with Chad and get on with our lives. We told them that we wanted the nightmare to be over with.

I am writing this book because God has shown us over and over that we are to tell his story. He has shown me Esther 4:14 many times: "If you keep quiet at a time like this, deliverance and relief from the Jews will arise from some other place, but you and your relatives will die. Who knows if perhaps you were made queen for just such a time as this?" (NLT).

I understand how people can question the existence of God especially in a world like ours today. However, after everything that Chad and I have been through, I know without a doubt that Jesus is real. I no longer have to "see it to believe it." My eyes and heart have been opened, and there is no turning back now!

I pray this book will shed light on how our Veterans are really treated. (There is a reason twenty-two a day commit suicide.) I pray this book will shed light on the truth about MRIs with contrast (gadolinium). I pray this story will bring hope to those who are desperate and searching for more.

> Yet what we suffer now is nothing compared to the glory he will reveal to us later. (Romans 8:18, NLT)

Naomi Ruth Thomas

Introduction

This is a trustworthy saying, and everyone should accept it: Christ Jesus came into the world to save sinners, and I am the worst of them all. But God had mercy on me so that Christ Jesus could use me as a prime example of his great patience with even the worst sinners. Then others will realize that they, too, can believe in him and receive eternal life.

—1 Timothy 1:15–16

I did not grow up in church. I did not grow up believing in God. I had no idea who Jesus was. I thought people who believed in God were crazy. I called them "Jesus Freaks." I was a terrible, terrible, terrible person. My family never went to church together. The only time God was mentioned was as a curse word. We grew up in what is considered the "Bible Belt," in North Carolina. I do not remember anyone really who I would have considered a true Christian. All I saw were a bunch of hypocrites.

In elementary school my teacher called my mom because of something that I had written in class. The question was, "What does your mother do for a living?" I answered that my mother was a bartender. The teacher told mom that obviously this was a mistake because our county was a "dry" county. My mom told her that it was not a mistake, that she was a bartender. My teacher told mom, "Well, I guess being a bartender isn't as bad as being a prostitute."

My name is Naomi Ruth, but not after the Bible. Ruth was my grandmother, and Naomi was a name from an awful poem that my mother remembered reading. My mother did not know that she was having twins until we were born, and I was a "surprise." I went to church several times with friends when I was younger, but it did not make sense to me. I did not know how people could believe in something that they could not see. Then, I met Jesus, and everything changed.

My twin sister, Arundel, and I went back to school in 2010 at the age of thirty because we wanted to become nurses. Our goal was to help Veterans. It is estimated that twenty-two Veterans a day commit suicide. Most recently in the news was the suicide of an army captain who was the thirtieth in his company to commit suicide. He was a Green Beret, he served six full tours in Afghanistan, and he committed suicide in front of his wife. He left behind three children. Arundel is an Air Force Veteran; my husband, Chad, is an Army Veteran; our brother is a Navy Veteran; our brother-in-law is a Marine Veteran; and my soon-to-be brother-in-law is a Coast Guard Veteran. Our grandfathers are Veterans, as well as cousins and friends.

At this point, in 2010, Chad had been dealing with untreated PTSD for five years. My plan was to get my bachelor's in nursing (BSN) and work for a Veterans Affairs (VA) Hospital. Ironically, it was at a VA hospital where this story begins.

I used to refer to what happened as a nightmare. It has been almost five years since this took place, and now I know that it was not a nightmare at all; it was a perfect storm. Chad went to a VA hospital for help, and everything that could possibly go wrong went wrong. But God was with us every second of every minute of every hour of every day. The only reason that Chad still has his leg and is alive today is because God allowed me to be a nurse.

I was forced to contact Congress, Senate, our local news, the White House, in addition to many, many others regarding what took place. We had seven meetings with the chief medical officer at the VA hospital, we saw over five "second opinion doctors," Chad had over seven different diagnoses, and it took thirteen months to find out what was wrong with Chad. We are thankful that it happened to us and not to another Veteran and his family. We have learned that everything happens for a reason; we are meant to help other Veterans, and we are meant to tell this story.

No one believes this story. To be honest, I still cannot believe that it happened to us either. But this is not our story, this is God's story. Only he can take credit for what happened. Chad and I started a website to try and tell this story. When I read it and look over the pictures, as a nurse I cannot believe that Chad is alive and still has his leg. When I read this story, I am in awe of our God! Our God is a God of miracles. A member at church said, "God doesn't do miracles anymore." When he said that, Chad and I almost fell out of our chairs. This story is filled with so many miracles, again it is hard to believe.

In the movie *The Case for Christ*, Lee Strobel states, "The only way to the truth is through facts. Facts are our greatest weapon against superstition, against ignorance, and against tyranny." We have facts, we have e-mails, pictures, text messages, medical records, recorded meetings, etc. These miracles cannot be denied because we have the facts, we have proof, and we have witnesses. What happened to us was life altering, it is mind-blowing, and all the glory goes to God!

I was thirty-six and a half years old when I resigned as a hospice nurse RN/BSN to take care of Chad full time; Chad was thirty-nine years old. To quote Chad's primary doctor, "His wife has advocated for him and in this way saved his life, not only from disease, but from suicide—which is where he was when I met him." This story is proof that our God is real and that Jesus is our ultimate Healer.

November 15, 2015

Chad was at a birthday party and was urged by family to go to the emergency room to get checked out. Chad had a large red bump on his right lower leg. We had been watching the spot and thought it was an infected hair follicle. There were several health professionals at the birthday party who agreed that Chad should be seen. Chad went to the Charles George VA Hospital Emergency Room in Asheville, North Carolina. He was told that his leg was possible MRSA. The physician's assistant came into the room with three to four nurses and a medical book. She said that Chad's leg was not MRSA; it was a spider bite.

The bump on Chad's leg measured 1 cm × 6 cm. Chad was diagnosed with a brown recluse spider bite sequela abscess. (*Sequela* means "a condition resulting from a prior disease, injury, or attack.") Chad's leg was I&D'd (incision and drainage); there was purulent drainage (pus), but no wound culture was done. Chad was given an IV antibiotic in the ER and sent home on antibiotics four times a day. Chad developed a progressive infection after the I&D. (When Chad returned home that night from the ER, he said he was not sure why, but he had a bad feeling that the PA messed his leg up.)

This picture is the morning after the I&D.

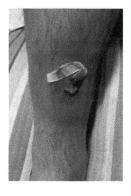

November 18, 2015

Chad was to return for a checkup after the I&D. Chad was enrolled at the Mountain Home VA Hospital in Tennessee and went there for his checkup. He was told that his leg was not a spider bite; it was cellulitis. He was to continue antibiotics four times and day and to follow up if needed.

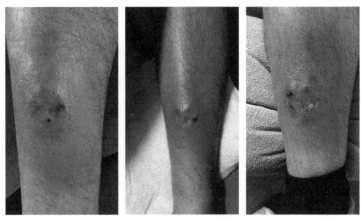

These pictures are Chad's leg from November 17–24.

November 24, 2015

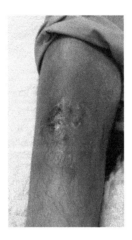

I showed pictures of Chad's leg to my hospice coworkers (ten-plus nurses, NP, etc.) and was told to take Chad back to the emergency room immediately. Chad and I went to the Charles George VA Emergency Room. Chad now had a wound that measured 15 cm × 14 cm. A wound culture was taken, and Chad was admitted to the hospital. An x-ray was taken of Chad's leg with no acute findings. Orthopedics and Surgery were consulted. Osteomyelitis (an infection of the bone) was suspected, and an MRI with contrast was performed.

Chad was admitted with the diagnosis of cellulitis, wound infection lower leg. The MRI showed "moderate subcutaneous enhancement involving the majority of the lower leg anterior to the tibia, likely representing Cellulitis. No evidence for Osteomyelitis."

Once Chad was admitted to the room, Wound Care was consulted. Wound Care came to see Chad's leg and said that Chad's "wound" was likely pyoderma gangrenosum (PG). According to the Mayo Clinic, "PG is a rare condition that causes large, painful sores to develop on your skin, most often the legs. No one knows exactly what causes pyoderma gangrenosum, but it is thought to be a disorder of the immune system."

The wound care doctor had seen *one* case of PG in his twenty-plus-year history and showed us pictures of the patient on his cell phone. In the medical record the doctor stated, "it is a bit late to biopsy him tonight." The doctor told us that he was doing a presentation in Florida on pyoderma gangrenosum and asked that I e-mail him pictures of Chad's leg for his presentation.

We were told by Wound Care that Chad's leg should not be debrided (the removal of damaged tissue) and nothing should be done surgically. We were told that debridement would make PG worse. We were told that Chad would *possibly* lose his leg and be in the hospital for weeks. We were told that Chad had no previous medical history or family history associated with PG. (The Wound Care nurse noted that about two days after the I&D, Chad reported new lesions were beginning in the pattern where local anesthetic was placed for the I&D and these began to drain purulent drainage and lesions were extremely painful.)

November 25–28, 2015

The next morning after admission, November 25, 2015, 7:55 a.m., Orthopedics came in to have Chad sign a consent form for surgery. Chad was to have surgery on Thanksgiving Day to have a bone sample taken and a wound vac placed. We informed the orthopedic doctor what the wound care doctor said the previous day and that we were told *nothing* surgically should be done at this time. Chad did *not* sign the consent form for surgery, and I went to find the nurse.

The nurse read the note from the wound care doctor and said that I was right; the doctor said nothing surgically should be done because it would make PG worse. I asked for the hospitalist to come to the room when she was available. (In the medical record, the Orthopedic doctor who tried to get Chad to sign the consent form for surgery wrote this: "Not sure why the lesion continues to worsen, given this fact, this could represent pyoderma gangrenosum, an inflammatory condition. Operative treatment of PG actually leads to continued wound advancement, so will need to give empiric antibiotic treatment to further delineate.")

In the medical record on the morning of November 26, 2015, Chad was scheduled to have right leg wound irrigation and debridement. They also had Chad tentatively scheduled for an I&D on November 27, 2015.

After the visit from the wound care doctor, the hospitalist changed Chad's diagnosis from *Right Anterior Shin Cellulitis* to *Wound likely pyoderma gangrenosum with superinfection.* Chad was given IV antibiotics while admitted and started on prednisone. We were told that prednisone would help with the redness and swelling but was not good for PTSD. Chad asked to speak to a mental health doctor while he was admitted.

After being told that Chad might possibly lose his leg and be in the hospital for weeks, Chad was discharged home on November 28, 2015. Chad was discharged with the diagnosis of *Pyoderma Gangrenosum and PTSD.* Chad was told to follow up with Wound Care and Rheumatology. We were told that the wound care doctor was booked three months out. The picture below is Chad's leg in the hospital before he was discharged.

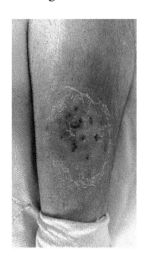

November 2015 through April 2016

Chad was under VA care at the Charles George VA Hospital for five months from November 2015 through April 2016. During this time, *no* autoimmune or genetic condition related to pyoderma gangrenosum was found. Chad had no family history or past medical history related to PG. The only testing done by Rheumatology was blood work. PG was thought to be associated with ulcerative colitis or Crohn's disease, yet no colonoscopy was ever performed.

The rheumatologist put Chad on methotrexate (chemotherapy medication) for "PG."   .

When I asked *why* Chad would be started on chemo medicine without further testing, we were told that methotrexate was a good choice for "PG," and it was a "weaker" form of chemotherapy. The doctor's note stated: "Would use methotrexate except he had a history of elevated liver enzymes which predicts a substantial risk that he would have to stop methotrexate because of further elevation of liver enzymes. Impression: *pyoderma gangrenosum.*"

Chad had an allergic reaction to the methotrexate. Within hours of the first dose, he had severe side effects. Chad would sweat profusely, his panic attacks increased dramatically as did his heart rate, anger, and rage. He had bumps pop up on his face and neck. The wound care doctor saw these new bumps and lanced several during an appointment. The doctor cultured one, said it was negative, and said the bumps *"were due to acne or inflammation."*

While under VA care, the wound care doctor began debriding Chad's leg for "PG." This is the *same* doctor who stated that debriding of PG would make it worse. Chad's leg was debrided every two weeks at first, even when his leg appeared to be healing. The wound care doctor did not come to several appointments, and Chad's leg was debrided by a plastic surgeon for "PG." The doctor who once was so excited about diagnosing "PG" now seemed uninterested. I communicated with the wound care doctor via e-mail, and I stopped hearing from him. Chad was still on prednisone (which decreases the immune system), and he was started on topical steroids for his leg. (This was in addition to the methotrexate prescribed by Rheumatology.) The original wound started to heal, and a new area of redness started to develop. I sent the hospitalist messages regarding the new area as well as the wound care doctor.

On April 11, 2016, we had an appointment with Primary Care, where I asked if Chad's leg looked like folliculitis (inflammation of the hair follicles).

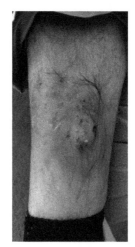

Chad's leg, April 11, 2016

We asked for referrals to an allergist and a dermatologist and were told to follow up with Wound Care and Rheumatology because it was "pyoderma gangrenosum." The referrals were denied, and Chad was told he was noncompliant for stopping the methotrexate.

After being denied referrals and Chad's leg continuing to get worse, we decided to go outside the VA for help. This appointment in April was the last time that we saw a VA doctor. (In addition to working full time as a hospice nurse, I was doing two to three dressing changes a day on Chad's leg. I was researching from the time I got home until midnight some nights trying to figure out what was wrong with Chad. My life revolved around keeping Chad alive.)

Going Outside the VA for Help

After speaking with my coworkers about Chad's situation, we contacted a local nurse practitioner (NP) who worked in Wound Care. He was shocked at methotrexate being used. He said that it was a "shotgun approach" that wiped out Chad's immune system. He said that Chad's leg could be "PG" but understood that PG is a diagnosis of *exclusion*. There are no specific tests/scans/x-rays/blood work that diagnoses PG; other things must be excluded before determining the diagnosis of PG. Chad had been on prednisone for six months at this time, and the NP wanted to get Chad off it.

The NP applied a wrap that was to be left on for three days to see if the swelling and redness would decrease. There was a slight decrease in redness after the wrap was removed, but then an infection started. The second appointment June 7, 2016, wound and bacterial cultures were taken, and Chad was started on two different antibiotics for an infection (Serratia). Chad took one antibiotic for two weeks, the other he was on for three weeks, and his leg continued to get worse.

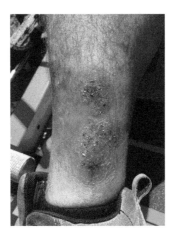

Side of Chad's leg

At this time, June 22, 2016, the NP said that it was honestly past his level of expertise and that he wanted to refer Chad to Infectious Disease. The NP had Chad continue with one antibiotic until he could get in to see Infectious Disease. The NP knew that Chad did not have outside insurance and suggested that we call the VA to tell them what was going on and to see if they could refer Chad to Infectious Disease. Chad was told he could stop taking prednisone after a final "prednisone burst" (eight months' total on prednisone).

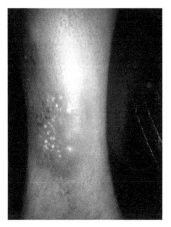

Side of Chad's leg

Contacting the VA

I called the Charles George VA on *June 29, 2016* and spoke to the nurse for Primary Care to inform her what was going on (the wound cultures, the antibiotics, the referral to Infectious Disease, Chad's leg continuing to get worse). The nurse spoke to the doctor and called me back. The nurse told me that the doctor said for Chad to follow up with Rheumatology because Chad had "PG." The doctor's note in the medical record states, "Patient has a history of pyoderma gangrenosum, for which he is being followed by rheumatology. According to records patient was a no show for rheumatology follow-up here on June 20th, 2016. Recommend patient to call rheumatology as soon as possible to reschedule follow-up appointment."

I called and spoke to a patient advocate at the VA. The advocate said that it was the Fourth of July weekend and that if I did not hear from anyone by July 5, 2016, to call back.

I never heard from anyone and called back on July 5, 2016. This time I spoke to a different patient advocate; *she was also a nurse.* I explained to her what was going on and about being denied the referral to Infectious Disease. She said that she remembered hearing about Chad's case from another advocate. She told me to send her the paperwork, and she would walk it personally to the chief medical officer as soon as I got it to her. I spent the day getting the proper paperwork sent from the outside NP with the referral to the patient advocate at the VA.

I never heard back from the patient advocate or anyone at the VA!

July 7, 2016: First Appointment with Infectious Disease

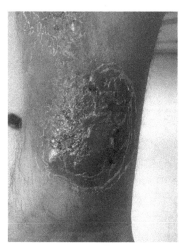

Side of Chad's leg, July 7, 2016

With Chad's leg continuing to get worse despite being on antibiotics for a month, we were desperate. We did not know how we would pay for the appointment, but we knew that something had to be done. The doctor was an hour and a half late to the appointment. We were told that she was a good doctor and that she would help us, so we waited patiently. I brought my photo album of Chad's leg, which at this time, eight months into this, had several hundred pictures.

The doctor looked through the pictures and said, "*It was obviously more complicated than originally thought.*" She said that a biopsy *must* be done to at least rule out cancer at this point. Chad had been on antibiotics for over a month, so we were told to come back in two weeks, and a biopsy would be done! The doctor had requested Chad's medical record from the VA but had not received it. I had my 418-page copy that I printed out at home, and I let her borrow it.

At the end of the appointment, the doctor informed us that her husband was also a doctor, and he worked at the Charles George VA Hospital. She said that he worked with the same doctors that Chad had been seeing (Rheumatology and Wound Care). We tried to remain optimistic, and we were excited about a biopsy finally being done! We thought, *Finally*, we are going to get to the bottom of this!

On July 20, 2016, I was contacted by the nurse practitioner who referred Chad to Mission Infectious Disease. The NP had spoken to the infectious disease doctor who informed the NP that *she had consulted the wound care doctor and the rheumatologist from the VA, and now she agreed with them that it was "PG" and that a biopsy was* not *necessary*. (Chad never authorized Infectious Disease contacting the VA). The nurse practitioner told me that he would do a biopsy if one was not done at our follow-up appointment.

After getting off the phone with the NP, I contacted the infectious disease doctor and left a message for her to please call me. The infectious disease doctor called to tell me that she had consulted three other physicians—the NP who referred us, the VA wound care doctor who had been seeing Chad, and the VA rheumatologist. She said that she thinks Chad's leg is "PG" and she is not 100 percent sure that a biopsy is necessary. She said the follow-up appointment was to determine *if* a biopsy was needed. I informed her that it was *not correct*; we were told (by her) that a biopsy would be done in two weeks after Chad had been off antibiotics. She told me that it was a "soft tissue" problem and for me to please reassure Chad that he would *not* lose his leg. ("PG" is *not* a soft tissue "problem.")

She asked that we please come to the follow-up appointment so she could explain things to us. The follow-up appointment was on July 25, 2016.

My Breaking Point

This is when I lost it! I was at work at the time. I went into the bathroom, projectile vomited, and almost blacked out. My CEO and nurse manager brought me into the office, and we discussed what was going on. They knew how terrible this all was and how Chad was continuing to get worse and that I was falling apart.

(Earlier in March, Chad was doing very badly, and I thought for sure that he would not survive. I was very desperate and hopeless and briefly thought about suicide. I did not tell Chad or Arundel about this; instead, I told my assistant nurse manager at Hospice. My manager made an appointment for me to see the doctor, and I was prescribed two different medications. The next doctor's appointment, my assistant manager went with me and did most of the talking for me because I could not. Our hospice CEO let me curl up in a ball on the floor in her office while we waited for my doctor's appointment. Our chaplain prayed for me and Chad and for our situation to get better.)

My CEO told me that they were going to raise one thousand dollars and that they were going to make Chad an appointment with a doctor who they *knew* would help us. After months of my coworkers telling me I needed to contact the congressman and the local news, I allowed them to do so. One coworker, a fellow nurse, contacted Congressman Mark Meadow's representative who called me the following day. She asked me to come up with a letter referencing what was going on and what we needed help with. I went home and wrote a fourteen-page letter.

On July 21, 2016, I sent my letter to Congress, Senate, other Veterans, pretty much anyone that I thought could help. (After writing my letter and referencing the patient advocate/nurse who was trying to help us, we were told by VA employees that she was transferred from the Charles George VA Hospital.)

Immediately after sending my letter to Senator Burr, we were contacted by the Charles George VA chief medical officer (CMO) to schedule an appointment. The appointment was scheduled for July 29, 2016.

My Letter Asking for Help

I am writing on behalf of my husband Richard Chad Thomas. My name is Naomi Thomas. I am 36 years old, and I live in Buladean, NC with my husband Chad and our four Old English Sheepdogs. I am a Registered Nurse (BSN) with Hospice of the Blue Ridge. I take care of people; it is my passion and my calling in life. Chad is 39 years old, has PTSD and does not currently work.

<u>We need your help getting Chad the mental health care he needs, and we need your help getting him quality and timely care of an on-going infection on his leg.</u>

Chad was in the Army from 2002 to 2006 and was an Airborne Infantryman. He was deployed to Iraq from 2004 to 2005 with an infantry unit assigned to the 525 Military Intelligence brigade where he was a Humvee gunner.

My husband is the best person in the whole world. He is my very best friend. Chad is kind, compassionate, handsome, hilarious, and he is great at everything he does. He is a beloved

31

husband, son, son-in-law, brother-in-law, uncle, grandson, and friend. More than anything, he is kind to others—he says hello and talks to everyone he sees at the VA Hospital. He Loves Veterans! He loves dogs as much as I do (and that is A LOT!) We have been together since we were kids, and I know him as well as I know myself. Sometimes I still cannot believe that he married me. He is so many wonderful things, but he used to be more. He used to love to make people laugh, he was a joker. He used to be an athlete, he used to love the outdoors and working out. He used to love life and look forward to what the day had to offer. He used to smile.

Chad has been home from Iraq for eleven years. He struggles with severe PTSD. He has as many as seven panic attacks a day and has been to the hospital with chest pain countless times. Most days, he is unable to leave the house. He doesn't do well in crowds. The panic attacks started not long after he got back from Iraq. He would get so upset about little things, things that I considered minor, and punch a hole in a door/wall. He would yell and scream and sweat. I had no idea what was going on. I know everyone thinks that families and soldiers going overseas are instructed on the signs/symptoms of PTSD, but that is not true. We were not instructed before he left, and we definitely were not after he came home. In the military asking for help is a sign of weakness, so no wonder why these soldiers are not asking for the help they need when they return. In the infantry world you are taught that crying, showing emotion and anything related to mental health are for the weak. You are taught to suck it up, rub some dirt on it and Charlie Mike (continue mission).

After getting out of the Army in 2006, Chad became a Sheriff's Deputy for six years. At first, he was so excited to be a Deputy and to have the chance to make a difference in the community. He did a good job trying to hide things for a while, but over time the stress became too much to bear. He would come home some nights and just explode. The stress was building and building, and I was worried that if he did not quit, he would have a heart attack or stroke, or that he would hurt someone or himself. Quitting was a very hard thing for him to do. It goes against everything he was taught. He was sick for days trying to just turn in his resignation letter. He felt like a failure, like he was letting his family down.

Chad is forever changed. He is not the same person I grew up with, and he is not the same person that I married. But he is still as important as ever, to me, to our family and friends, and to our dogs. He is still the same loving, wonderful guy, but he needs help. He is not getting that help. This has been a very frustrating experience, trying to get him the help that he needs. I won't give up—we will continue to fight, and when we don't get the help we need, we will fight harder. When Chad is worn out and wants to give up, I will fight for him. He would do the same thing for me, no question. I need help. Chad needs help. We cannot do this alone, but we have not received the help from the VA that we need. Specifically, we need help with mental health treatment, and we need help with treatment for his leg.

As this point, we are just exhausted, depressed, hopeless, and frustrated. We really need some help. Chad is not getting the care he needs from the VA. We desperately need a diagnosis. He needs consistent, quality mental health care. This situation is negatively impacting our lives in many ways. Chad is currently more depressed than ever. I have become obsessed with his leg and have become depressed and angry. Sometimes taking care of Chad is a full-time job. Some days are really hard. I have been unable to focus while at work, concerned for my husband's physical and mental health. He deserves better than this.

Thank you for reading this letter. I know that it is long and contains a lot of detail, but I hope that it has made clear that our experience dealing with obtaining mental health care and wound care through the VA has been a challenging, frustrating, and ultimately negative experience. To recap, we are respectfully requesting prioritized mental health care for Chad, with regular, quality visits with a psychiatrist in a one-on-one setting, or an opportunity for inpatient mental health care. Additionally, we are requesting approval to obtain service from an infectious disease doctor to determine the cause of his leg wound.

I would like to close with a few pictures of Chad's leg today 7/17/16 (8 months since this started), as I am finishing typing this paper.

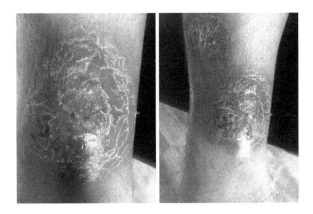

In this letter I included the details of Chad's leg wound and our experience dealing with the Charles George VA Hospital. I did not include all that because it is explained in great detail throughout this story, and I do not want to repeat myself.

Just Give It to God

One of my hospice patients told me that he heard God speak to him. He had been a truck driver for over fifty years, and at the age of seventy-six, he heard God call his name and tell him to get off the road. I thought he was crazy and did not know what to chart for his mental status. I wondered if he was "all there," maybe he suffered from dementia. I just could not believe what he was telling me. I had never seen or heard God before or heard anyone else say anything like this. Then, I saw *God* in another one of my hospice patients.

Everyone, including my patients, could see me falling apart before their eyes. I was desperate as Chad continued to get worse, and I consulted everyone that I could, including my patients. My patient knew what Chad and I were going through, and she kept telling me to "give it to God." I had no idea what she was talking about.

Here was a woman who was dealing with a terrible disease. She was given five years to live, and that was over twenty-three years ago! Because of her disease, she had to have all her teeth removed, she was losing her eyesight, she had to have four fingers removed, most days she was unable to leave her house, she was on oxygen, etc. She had so many reasons that she could be bitter, but she was not. She talked to me about Jesus, and even though I did not know who *he* was, I saw *him* in her.

The first time I met her, she told me that she felt like she had known me her whole life, and I felt the same way. There was a peace about her that I did not understand. There was a joy about her that I could not wrap my head around. I had never met anyone like her. We lived five minutes from each other, but until then, we had never met. God sent her into my life for a reason. I was at my lowest point, and she was just what I needed. She and her husband would talk to me about God every time I was at their house.

The Day I Gave It to God

On July 22, 2016, I "gave it to God." I surrendered. I realized that I am not in control; it hit me like a ton of bricks. I had spent my whole life (I was thirty-six and a half years old) searching for something, knowing that something was missing. By the world's standards, I had every reason to be happy. I was married to the love of my life, my high school sweetheart who was my best friend, and I had an identical twin sister who was also my best friend. I had a great job as a nurse (RN/BSN), I was making good money, I thought I had things all figured out. I felt empty inside, and I did not know why. I was angry, mean, selfish, and spoiled. *I wanted what I saw in my patient.* I wanted that joy and peace that I saw in her.

My life changed that day, but not just my life changed, my twin sister Arundel was saved soon after, and we were baptized together in the river. Chad's life changed too because of what he saw in me. (He rededicated his life to Christ in 2017 and was baptized).

Arundel is on the left, and I am on the right.

The *same* day that I was saved, my patient wrote me this note in a prayer journal she gave me. This is her note:

> My Heart, Naomi, Precious One, **God** has a promise for your every need. Our **God** created you the great someone you are! A heart so full of love and with giving compassion. You are admired and loved and a most wonderful nurse. Will always treasure you in my heart!

She signed her name and wrote Philippians 4:13: "I can do all things through Christ who gives me strength."

After giving it to God, things started changing *immediately*!

July 25th, 2016: Follow-Up Appointment with Infectious Disease

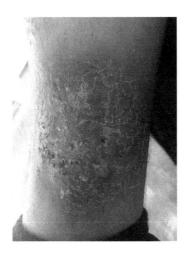

We listened to the infectious disease doctor as she told us about consulting the VA doctors. She told us that she now believed Chad's leg was "PG" and that a biopsy should *not* be done. We thanked her and told her that we came to her for help; we were referred to her because it was past Wound Care's expertise.

Chad's leg was awfully bad at this time and draining pus. I asked her if she would do a MRSA swab on the drainage. *She told us that a MRSA swab was a waste of money.* I asked her to please do one. She cultured Chad's leg and then told us that we did not need Infectious Disease; we needed Dermatology. We had already informed her that we asked for a dermatologist from the VA and were denied. Her discharge diagnosis for Chad was *PTSD and PG*.

(The next week the doctor called to tell us that the culture came back *positive for Staph*. She said that she did not think that Chad needed to be on antibiotics, and she did not think the underlying reason was infection.)

There Is Hope!

The next day, July 26, 2016, we had our first appointment with Dr. Kelly Rothe in Burnsville, North Carolina. Hospice of the Blue Ridge raised one thousand dollars and made the appointment for us. Dr. Rothe had requested the letter that I wrote, our pictures, Chad's 418-page medical record, everything that we had before our first visit.

Our appointment was three hours long, and she did a biopsy on the first visit! Dr. Rothe had a medical student training with her that day. She told the medical student, "*Please don't treat people like this. Don't make people go to these great lengths, just do a biopsy.*"

When we first met Dr. Rothe, we had already figured that Chad was going to lose his leg. We had been told this from the VA, and Chad's leg was getting worse; it seemed to be spreading up and around. We decided that if it spread to a certain point (we were measuring it and had it marked), Chad would go ahead and have his leg removed. We thought at least this way that we could get on with our lives. We informed Dr. Rothe about being okay with Chad losing his leg, and she looked puzzled. She told us that she did *not* think that Chad would lose his leg! We finally saw some hope after dealing with this for eight months without answers.

July 29th, 2016: First Meeting with the Charles George VA Chief Medical Officer (CMO)

Our first meeting was with the chief medical officer (CMO) and the risk management nurse. They asked us what we wanted and briefly asked about mental health. We were told that they were *very* concerned about Chad's leg and that we needed to come up with a plan for treatment. The risk management nurse told us that she had *no* knowledge of Chad's case/file, *but she would be doing an extensive review into it.* We were told that Chad should not be admitted to the hospital because the risk of infection was too high. We were told that if Chad needed IV antibiotics, this could be done at home.

We were asked if Chad wanted to continue seeing Wound Care and Rheumatology at the VA, and Chad said *no*. The CMO said they could refer Chad to Dermatology; they had three good dermatologists at the VA. We told them about asking for referrals to Dermatology and an allergist and being denied. We told them that the only doctor who "seemed to even care" while Chad was admitted was the hospitalist. We told them about Hospice raising one thousand dollars and our appointment with Dr. Rothe. We told them that a biopsy had *finally* been done, and we were waiting for the results! They did not ask to see Chad's leg. Chad showed them his leg so they could see what we were dealing with.

Mental Health

After sending my letter to Congressman Mark Meadows and Senator Burr, we were contacted by a mental health doctor at the Charles George VA Hospital. The doctor said that her boss had received my letter from Senator Burr, and she was told to see Chad and I personally for counseling. During our first appointment, she congratulated me on writing my letter and for being a patient advocate for Chad. She urged us to continue to fight!

We saw the doctor several times for counseling as Chad's leg continued to get worse. It was over an hour's drive each way, and the doctor mentioned that we could do telehealth visits where we could speak over the computer. She also mentioned that the CMO and others could have access to the telehealth portal and could listen in. We were not comfortable with this at all. Dr. Rothe helped Chad and I get set up with the Wounded Warrior Project (WWP), and we received counseling outside of the VA Health System for over a year.

August 2, 2016: Resigning from Hospice of the Blue Ridge

I had a three-hour meeting with my CEO, CFO, HR, assistant manager, and nurse manager. They tried to do everything possible to help. They offered me a smaller workload with less patients and less hours. They asked me to be honest with them whether I would be able to do this. I thought about it for a minute and then, with my head down and tears running down my face, I told them that I could not handle it. I was barely hanging on as it was. Chad was continuing to get worse, and taking care of him was a full-time job. They donated over 270 PTO hours for me so that I would continue to have a paycheck and health insurance while we were struggling so badly. *With a heavy heart, I headed home to talk to Chad about what was going on.*

On my way home, I received a phone call from a Vietnam Veteran who has been my friend for a long time. He was one of the *many* people that I sent my letter to. He told me that the chief medical officer would be receiving a phone call from Washington DC that day *and to expect a phone call.* (My friend had sent the letter I wrote to a lot of people asking for help, and one of these people is a general who works at the Pentagon.)

Not long after arriving home, the risk management nurse called from the VA to schedule an appointment with us. She scheduled the appointment for August 11th. A little while later, we received another phone call from the VA, this time it was the CMO. He saw where Risk Management scheduled an appointment and wanted to see if we could meet sooner. Meeting number 2 was scheduled for the following day, August 3, 2016.

Bullies No Bueno

After sending my letter to Congress and Senate, we were bombarded by calls from the VA hospital. The CMO, Dr. Bazemore (who is a bully), would call us all the time. Dr. Rothe had to call the CMO and tell him to leave us alone. We were told to leave the phone off the hook during the day to avoid being harassed.

Before becoming CMO, Dr. Bazemore oversaw the ICU at the Charles George VA Hospital. He was the doctor in charge when Sgt. Powell was given the incorrect amount of Dilaudid several times, without being on a monitor. Sgt. Powell did not survive.

August 3rd, 2016: Second Meeting with the Charles George VA

A patient advocate met us at the door of the executive suite and walked us down to the CMO's office and introduced us to the CMO (even though we had already met). This time, in addition to the CMO and risk management nurse was the hospitalist that we *mentioned* during our first meeting.

We were told by the CMO that they were *very worried* about Chad and they felt that this needed to be taken care of *immediately*. They said the best idea would be to get all care (mental health and treatment of Chad's leg) under one roof. We were told that Chad could be admitted back to the Charles George VA and *they would take care of everything*, or we could try to go to the VA in Durham. They were unsure how long it would take to get into the Durham VA. *They told us that the decision was ours to make, but we needed to go ahead and decide.*

After much thought and feeling pressured, Chad told them that he would be okay with being readmitted to the Charles George VA and give them another shot. I had to speak up and asked *if* Chad were readmitted *what the plan was*. They said that they were going to run tests and get a dermatologist on board.

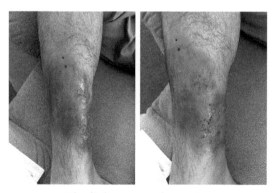

Chad's leg, second meeting

We told them that we were waiting for the biopsy results that Dr. Rothe took on July 26, 2016. We were told by the risk management nurse that the biopsy results *"really don't matter."* We were told that *"the biopsy was probably just going to come back as dead tissue, and if we were putting all our hopes on the biopsy determining a diagnosis, that we need to* accept that the biopsy isn't going to do this."

We were told that we needed to *"accept the fact that it is the diagnosis* they *said it is, we needed to accept that Chad might lose his leg and that Chad is going to have to take medications that he doesn't want to take for the rest of his life."* We were told that Chad would probably have to go back on prednisone and methotrexate. They said they would run tests and do blood work, but they wanted us to know that even when they do all this, we need to realize and accept that it is the original diagnosis of "PG."

Chad told them that he was worried about his leg, but he was really worried about me! He told them about me resigning from my job to take care of him full time. We just wanted the nightmare to be over with. We did not know what to do.

After agreeing to be readmitted the following day to the Charles George VA Hospital, the CMO was *so* happy. He noticed a tattoo on Chad's arm of "Dirty Harry" that he had not seen the first appointment. With a huge smile on his face, the CMO told Chad, "You know what, you just made my day!"

We headed home and felt *very uneasy about things.* Chad was to be readmitted the next day at noon. We were told by the CMO that he would be a direct admission, and they would take care of everything.

Phone Calls from the VA after the Second Meeting

After the second meeting, Chad and I headed home to pack for Chad to be admitted the following day. The first phone call we received was from Non-VA Care. He told us Chad was *not* to be admitted to the Charles George VA; he was to go to Duke (Durham VA). We informed Non-VA Care of our appointment with the CMO and what we were told about a direct admission the following day. He said he would investigate it and call us back.

Next, we received a phone call from the doctor in charge of inpatient admissions. He said basically he was told that Chad was going to be a direct admission and did not have to go through the ER. He asked *who* told us this, and I told him it came from the CMO. The doctor in charge of admissions said that even though we were told this, there weren't any beds available and Chad would have to wait in the ER until a room became available and he honestly had no idea how long it would be.

The Biopsies Came Back!

It was at this point that Chad and I really started getting worried. I called Hospice to speak to my coworkers to tell them what was going on and to ask their advice. My assistant nurse manager suggested that I call Dr. Rothe's office to let them know what happened at the meeting. I called Dr. Rothe's office and asked to speak to the nurse. I knew that Dr. Rothe was out of town, but I had to tell them what was going on and about Chad being readmitted to the Charles George VA or possibly Duke. Dr. Rothe's nurse said she really wanted to get in touch with Dr. Rothe, but she was on vacation. I told her that we did not want to bother Dr. Rothe; we just did not know what to do.

While we were on the phone, the nurse happened to check the computer, and Chad's biopsy results had just come in! Dr. Rothe had not seen the results yet, so the nurse had to speak with the PA and then call us back.

After having our meeting with the VA, where we were told that the biopsy results "really don't matter," Dr. Rothe's nurse called back and said, "*We finally have a diagnosis!*" She told me that both biopsies came back as *panniculitis*. I had no idea what that was, but Chad and I remembered Dr. Rothe mentioning panniculitis *during the first appointment*. The nurse printed the results out and told us to come by the office on our way home and pick them up. The nurse said that she left a message for Dr. Rothe even though she was on vacation; she knew that Dr. Rothe would want to know about the biopsy results and the VA wanting to readmit Chad.

The VA

After leaving Dr. Rothe's office (with the biopsy results in hand), we received another phone call from Non-VA Care (third phone call from the VA since leaving the appointment).

We were told by Non-VA Care that he had heard from the CMO twice, once by phone and once by e-mail, and Chad was *not* to be admitted to the Charles George VA; he was to go to Duke (Durham VA).

As soon as we got home, I called the risk management nurse and left a message. I called the CMO and left a message with his secretary for him to please call me back. The CMO called back on our home phone, and at the exact same time Dr. Rothe called my cell phone. I told Dr. Rothe that the CMO was on the phone, and she said she would call back. I told the CMO that I really needed to talk to Dr. Rothe *because the biopsy results were in, and we had a diagnosis!* I also told the CMO about Non-VA Care calling and the doctor in charge of admissions. The CMO said it was all just a miscommunication.

The CMO asked what the biopsy results were. I told him that I was *not* comfortable telling him until we had a chance to speak to Dr. Rothe. He asked if Chad was still going to be admitted the following day, and I told him that I did not know; we needed to speak to Dr. Rothe.

Dr. Rothe

Dr. Rothe, who was on vacation, called back and asked about the biopsy results.

I read her the results: both biopsies came back as *Fibrosing Panniculitis with lipomembranous foci.* (*Panniculitis* is inflammation of the subcutaneous fat.) I was on the phone with Dr. Rothe for a while, and she said that Chad should *not* be admitted to Duke (Durham VA) *or* the Charles George VA. She said she would work on a detailed plan of care as soon as she returned from her vacation. Dr. Rothe ended up coming home early from her vacation to work on this for Chad.

Chad Will Not be Admitted to the VA

First thing the next morning, I called the VA to let them know that Chad would *not* be admitted. I also sent the CMO an e-mail explaining that Dr. Rothe said admission was not necessary, since we *now* had biopsy results *and* a diagnosis. That morning, starting at 7:11 a.m. and going until 8:00 p.m., we received text messages, sixteen-plus phone calls, and e-mails from the VA. I received a text message from the hospitalist asking what the biopsy results were.

My letter to the CMO and risk management nurse:

> Good morning,
>
> As I told the CMO yesterday afternoon, the biopsy results are back and I had a very long detailed conversation with Dr Kelly Rothe last night—who called me from her vacation because she got a message about yesterday's events and is very concerned.
>
> **Chad will not be coming today to be admitted.** We have a lot of things to figure out right now. Dr Rothe said that going in patient or being transferred to Duke in an unnecessary expense. She recommends many things, as I tried to get across yesterday in our meeting.
>
> I do not know what all is going to happen, I do not know at this point WHO ALL we need to contact.
>
> I do not know if either of you read my letter, but Dr Rothe who we met one time—for a 3-hour visit—read my letter and made extensive notes from it and ended up doing a biopsy

immediately—has sent my letter to many people as well.

We were told yesterday by Kim Pierce that we need "**to accept that the biopsy results are not going to be the determining factor and will not give us a definite diagnosis**." The biopsy is just going to be dead tissue is what we were told by Kim Pierce and Dr Ruiz.

I am sure that Kim has lot more experience than I do, I see that she has her MSN. I only have my BSN, but I AM A PATIENT ADVOCATE. I am my husband's advocate and like I said from the start, **THIS IS NOT PG**!!

I know that Kim had no knowledge of this case when we met on Friday. She said she was going to do an "intense review of Chad's medical record to see where things went wrong". I am looking forward to that. I am actually excited about someone doing that. I have been told that this is already being done. Believe me, I have been doing that this entire time.

We have not been impressed with the lack of knowledge from all parties included in this case/struggle/nightmare, whatever you want to call it.

If you would like me to send you my latest email that has already been sent out, I would be glad to. Please just let me know. We have been through enough. In 11 days, it will be 9 months since the initial "spider bite" ER visit.

I know that Washington is watching, I know that the Pentagon is watching. I know that so many others are watching this as well.

I am embarrassed that the "VA SYSTEM" has led Chad and I to the breaking point. I have been told not to apologize, to be proud of myself for the love and compassion that I have shown for standing up for MY SOLDIER!!!!!!!

I will say after the events from yesterday, I honestly do not know what needs to happen. I am truly embarrassed that this is how our Veterans are treated!!!!!!

My gut instinct is to say I am sorry, but I should not be the one apologizing at this point.

My husband WHO DOES NOT CRY, was in tears yesterday after the meeting and the following 3 phone calls we received from the Charles George VA after we left the appointment.

All I know as of 9:35 am is this—Chad will **not** be coming today to be admitted to the Charles George VA and will not need to go to Duke at this time.

I understand that healthcare is changing, and the VA system has always been like this, or so I have heard from all these people since my letter went out. But, if something is broken, instead of putting a band aid on it, why not try to fix it?

This experience has changed every single thing about our life. I am tired of crying; I am tired of begging for help. I want Chad to get treatment, but it should be the CORRECT TREATMENT.

I will be sending this letter and my letter that I wrote at 4:55 am this morning (because once again I am so upset that I cannot sleep) to many people today.

I feel like we have given the VA almost 9 months to figure this out. Chad told me yesterday that he really felt that if he were to be admitted to your hospital, that there is no doubt he would end up losing his leg. Now, of course that is his opinion and after all of this, he is free to feel whatever and however he wants to feel.

Once we figure out a game plan and the next step, someone will be in contact with you.

Naomi Ruth Thomas

I spoke to the CMO on Friday, August 5, 2016, and told him that Dr. Rothe was coming home early from her vacation and was working on a detailed plan of care. She would be back into town on the 9th.

We had our second appointment with Dr. Rothe on August 10, 2016, and returned home around 7:00 p.m. At 8:07 p.m., the CMO called. He asked what the diagnosis was and what the biopsy showed. I told him that Dr. Rothe was working on her detailed plan and would have it to us ASAP. Chad had a mental health appointment the next day, and we told him we would come by afterward to see him. Dr. Rothe hurried to finish the plan of care so we could take it with us to our appointment the following day with the CMO. The CMO asked *who* we wanted to be at the third meeting, and we said just him would be fine.

August 11, 2016: Third Meeting with the Charles George VA Hospital CMO

Dr. Rothe came up with an incredibly detailed fourteen-point plan of care for Chad's leg and mental health that we brought with us to the appointment. The CMO asked what we wanted to do about Chad's leg, and we explained that Dr. Rothe had come up with a plan. He skimmed over her paperwork and asked what was being done for Chad's leg *now*? (At this point, Dr. Rothe had already done the biopsy, Chad had genetic testing done as well as pulmonary function tests and an ultrasound to his leg to rule out a blood clot. This was within two appointments with Dr. Rothe.) The CMO asked Chad if he wanted to see Wound Care and Rheumatology, and Chad again said no.

The CMO briefly scanned over Dr. Rothe's plan of care and saw where she had written:

It is a type of Panniculitis (inflammation of the subcutaneous fat). Reassured this is not near the bone or muscle so no cause to think you will lose your leg.

The CMO told us that he "*didn't think anyone at the VA had ever told Chad that he might lose his leg.*" I told him that this was *not* correct. We had been told that since the original misdiagnosis of "PG" in November 2015, and we were also told that in our second meeting with him!

Dr. Rothe's Plan of Care

Dr. Rothe came up with an incredibly detailed fourteen-point plan of care for Chad after receiving the biopsy results of panniculitis. As previously stated, we brought this with us to our third meeting with the CMO.

Some of her main points from the plan of care were as follows:

- Chad's PTSD "was exacerbated further by seven months of steroid use which progressed his anxiety to angry outbursts, suicidal thoughts, and self-injury.
- "Anxiety over VA appointment last week where **was told he will likely lose his leg** and feeling pressured to go back into the hospital for IV steroids and methotrexate despite his reaction to both of these medications and failure to note improvement."
- "Did you ever have a colonoscopy? Given relation of skin disorder to ulcerative colitis or Crohn's may be helpful to know."
- "It is a type of panniculitis (inflammation of subcutaneous fat). **Reassured this is not near bone or muscle so no cause to think you will lose your leg.**
- "To promote local wound healing of superinfections (has had serratia and staph aspirated from bulla) considered Wound care center for hyperbaric chamber therapy but Dr Humphries said he cannot/will not do hyperbaric chamber for inflammatory disease especially with panic disorder because it takes three hours in the chamber—Chad agrees to do other things to prevent superinfection."
- "At this point agree you are disabled, recommend hiring a lawyer to get your SSI, and having VA evaluate for 100% disability. However, do remain hopeful within a couple of years we will be able to get you better, and volunteering

in organizations you love will help you feel part of a community and prevent the depression associated with PTSD and isolation. If you have GI bill options for school I recommend using this as able one class at a time until better to educate yourself for a job that does not require trauma, death, etc. anything that will retrigger your stress reactions."

Chad's Leg Continued to Get Worse

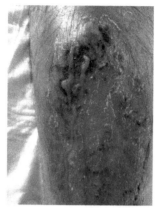

Mid-August, Chad's leg continued to get worse, and Dr. Rothe did a wound culture. The lab misread the report, said it was MRSA, and Chad was started on antibiotics. When Dr. Rothe received the report, she realized that it was not MRSA; it was Staph, and Chad was told he could stop the antibiotics. Chad's leg seemed to get worse while he was on antibiotics.

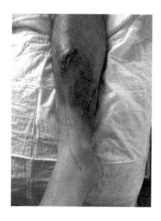

Wake Forest Dermatology

The first biopsies that were done by Dr. Rothe were sent to Quest Diagnostics. The pathologist and Dr. Rothe communicated several times regarding Chad's case. Dr. Rothe called the pathologist before the biopsies were taken to inform him that it was eight months without a biopsy and asked where the biopsies should be taken from.

The pathologist was associated with Wake Forest and said he was sending Chad's slides and case to Wake Forest Dermatology. Chad and I were contacted by Wake Forest Dermatology as well as Dr. Rothe. They were having a physicians' clinical conference (a round table of doctors, the head of Dermatology, Pathology, etc.). We were asked to sit in on the conference while they discussed Chad's case. It was not an exam; it was a conference (no fee), and they would discuss options and come up with a plan. Dr. Rothe was invited to the conference as well.

I was asked to come up with a timeline for the conference. I was asked to pick several of the worst pictures from each month and figure out what medications Chad was taking at the time, what was going on, etc. This took me several days to go through and figure out what medicines he was on and relate them to the appropriate pictures. When I was finished, I sent this to Dr. Rothe who was going to share it with Wake Forest.

We told the CMO at the Charles George VA about the biopsies being sent to Wake Forest. He asked *why* they were sent to Wake Forest. The CMO asked if Dr. Rothe went to school at Wake Forest and wanted to know why exactly they were sent there. We told the CMO about the upcoming physicians' clinical conference at Wake Forest and that it was a free appointment and no exam was being done that day. The CMO said he would send the proper paperwork to Wake Forest in case they wanted to admit Chad. He said that he was taking care of everything.

The week of the appointment with Wake Forest, we were contacted because they had not received anything from the Charles George VA regarding preapproval in case Chad needed to be admitted. I contacted the CMO who told me that he did *not* say they were paying for anything and that I told him the appointment was free. After a long, frustrating discussion, the CMO said he would contact Wake Forest.

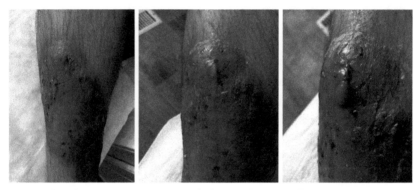

The above pictures are Chad's leg at the end of August 2016.

September 14, 2016: The Day of the Physicians' Clinical Conference at Wake Forest

Chad and I drove down to Winston Salem with family the night before the appointment and spent the night. It was about a six-hour roundtrip drive and we wanted to be there first thing and not be stressed. Dr. Rothe was not able to make the appointment because of work obligations.

We were brought into an exam room where they explained that doctors/medical students would be coming in to ask questions, take pictures, etc., and we were not to tell them what was wrong with Chad's leg. They could ask questions, but we were not to tell them about the biopsy results and give too much detail. *Nothing at all was mentioned about the physicians' clinical conference!* Thirty to forty-plus medical students came in to look at Chad's leg, ask questions, take pictures, etc. After that, we were told they were finished and we could go home. We were in shock!

We were about five minutes down the road, and we were called to come back because they wanted to do a biopsy on Chad's leg. They did two biopsies; the doctor was not sure where to do them on Chad's leg and did an older area on the side. When she did the biopsy, she was surprised when pus came out and did a wound culture on the drainage. The doctor put the reason for the biopsy was a "rash" on Chad's leg. We were told that the biopsies were done in house and it would take about two weeks to get the results back. I called after two weeks and was told that the results were abnormal and were sent off for more slides.

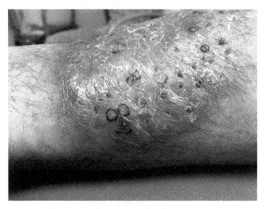

The doctor drew this on Chad's leg before the biopsies were taken.

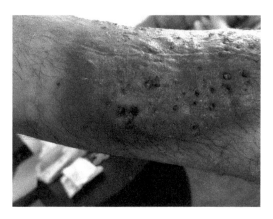

September 16th, 2016: Fourth Meeting with the Charles George VA Hospital

This was our fourth meeting with the CMO. In attendance on this meeting was the director of the Charles George VA Hospital, CMO, a nurse, Chad, myself, my twin sister, and my mother.

Chad asked the director of the Charles George VA what she would do if this happened to her. The director said she would listen to her doctor and do what they told her to do. Chad was told that he needed to do what the doctors told him to do, that he was a non-compliant patient.

He was told to pick a doctor, stick with the doctor, and do what the doctor tells him to do.

We informed them that Chad has done everything he has been told to do and that Dr. Rothe is his doctor and Chad has done everything she has told him to do.

After the meeting, we were told by the CMO to go to Caregiver Support and meet with the social worker. The CMO told us that I qualify for the caregiver program as a nurse taking care of Chad full time, and we would get set up in the program and I would receive a paycheck. (They knew that I resigned to take care of Chad full time.) We met with the social worker who told me that I did not qualify for the program. He said that he did not know *why* we were meeting; he just wanted to meet us face to face because he had heard about us.

After the fourth meeting and while we were waiting for the latest biopsy results from Wake Forest, we were contacted by the social worker we met with from the caregiver program. He asked me how Chad's leg was doing; he asked what the latest biopsy results were from Wake Forest. I told him that the biopsy results were not back yet. He asked me *who* our contact person was at Wake Forest; I told him that we did not have a contact person. He asked *how* Wake Forest got in contact with us regarding the biopsy results and if they contacted us directly or if they went through Dr. Rothe. I told him that they contacted Dr. Rothe.

After our fourth meeting, the director of the Charles George VA Hospital sent Senator Burr and Congressman Mark Meadows a letter about Chad's case. I was contacted by the Congressman's representative after they received the letter to ask if it was accurate and where things stood. Here are some of the things the director of the hospital wrote to the senator and congressman:

Thank you for your inquiry on behalf of Naomi Thomas regarding the management of the medical care for her husband, Chad Thomas. I regret that their prior experience with VA healthcare has not met their expectations. Since reviewing this inquiry, we have been attempting to work with the Thomas' to address his various health needs, but we have been unable to reach a mutually agreeable plan of care to this point. In an effort to establish a definitive course of action, I, along with (Chief of Staff), and Mr. and Mrs. Thomas, met on September 16th, 2016. I expressed my hope that Dr. Rothe, a community provider they have been seeing, and a clinical team at Wake Forest would be able to determine the cause and cure for Mr. Thomas' leg wound. In closing, I reiterated that we are most concerned that Mr. Thomas receives the best care directed toward treatment of his leg and strongly encouraged him to follow through with the care plan formulated by the physicians from Wake Forest. Thank you for your interest in the well-being of our nation's Veterans. I trust that this response has sufficiently addressed your concerns.

The biopsies taken by Wake Forest took longer than expected; they said the results were abnormal and being sent off for more slides. When the results finally came back, we were told they were all normal. We were told that both biopsies came back as ruptured follicular cysts.

October 25, 2016: Second Appointment with Wake Forest Dermatology

A doctor we had not met on the first appointment asked us questions to bring him up-to-date from November 2015 through October 2016. We told him about the first biopsies, panniculitis, Serratia, Staph times 2, Chad's leg continuing to get worse, the latest biopsy results of ruptured follicular cysts, etc.

The doctor left and returned with another doctor we had not met during the first visit. The doctor walked in, glanced at Chad's legs, and immediately said it was pyoderma gangrenosum.

I asked the doctor why she said pyoderma gangrenosum immediately on walking into the room and glancing at Chad's legs. She said it was "PG" because both legs were affected. We told her about panniculitis and how Chad's left leg started as an infected hair follicle, but she was not listening to what we were telling her. She spent five to ten minutes in the room with us. She asked if Chad tried prednisone for "PG." We informed her that Chad had been on prednisone for eight months without improvement. The doctor said that Chad needed to be started on Humira for "PG." (Humira is an immunosuppressive drug; it is used to treat arthritis, Crohn's disease, and ulcerative colitis. Humira suppresses the immune system and increases the chance of getting infections.) We told the doctor that Chad did not need Humira. Chad had several infections during this time and did not need any more, and we knew it was not "PG."

The doctor said that Chad needed a wrap on his leg for "PG." She said the wrap was to be left on for a week, and then we could remove it. Within thirty minutes of the wrap being applied to Chad's leg, his leg started burning. I called back and left a message for the nurse about the burning. We did not hear from them, so I contacted Dr. Rothe. I informed her about the appointment and that a wrap was applied, and we were told to leave it on for a week. We returned home, and Chad had the wrap on for five hours and could not take the burning anymore.

Dr. Rothe instructed us to remove the wrap immediately. We removed the wrap, and after five hours, Chad had a first-degree burn from the wrap!

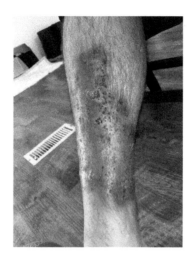

October 27, 2016: Fifth Appointment with the Charles George Hospital CMO

After returning home from Wake Forest, the CMO called to ask how the appointment went at Wake Forest and what was done.

Chad told the CMO about the wrap being applied for "PG" and about it burning. Chad told him that we took the wrap off and the CMO asked why. We informed him that it was burning and we were instructed to take it off by Dr. Rothe after it had been on for five hours. The CMO said he was going to contact Wake Forest and speak to the doctor we saw that day. Meeting number 5 was scheduled with the CMO for October 27, 2016.

* * * * *

This meeting was the worst so far. It was just the CMO, Chad, and me. The CMO told us that he had spoken to the doctor that we saw at Wake Forest who applied the wrap for "PG." The CMO said that doctor was highly intelligent and seemed to know her stuff. The CMO said that we should really listen to the doctor from Wake Forest and stick with her. We informed the CMO that we were *not* impressed by the doctor, that she walked in and immediately said it was "PG"; when asked why she said "PG," she said because both legs were involved. She spent five to ten minutes with Chad, she didn't know about the biopsies being taken, she asked if Chad tried prednisone—when he was on it for eight months; she took her cell phone out and took pictures of Chad's leg, etc.

The CMO told Chad he was noncompliant for taking off the wrap even though it was burning (it caused a first-degree burn and was instructed to be removed by Dr. Rothe). The CMO told Chad that he needed to pick a doctor and stick with them. Chad informed him that he had Dr. Rothe and he was doing everything she told him to do. We informed the CMO about the social worker calling the house, asking about the latest biopsy results and who our contact person was at Wake Forest. We told the CMO that it was weird that a doctor we had never seen walked right in, glanced at Chad's legs, and immediately said it was "PG." We told him that it seemed like someone had told her what to say. The CMO said the only time he had contacted Wake Forest was after the appointment when the wrap was applied. Chad told the CMO that it all started with the "spider bite" in the ER November 2015.

The CMO said *"Spider bite? What spider bite?"* He said, "That happened at the VA in TN, *not* here." We informed the CMO that it happened at his hospital. He started getting upset, and we said the meeting was over.

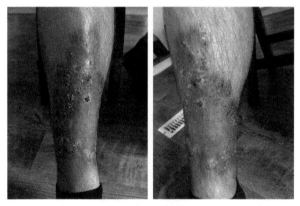

Pictures were taken the day of our fifth meeting with the CMO.

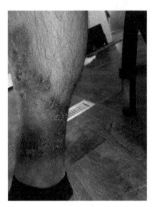

Side of leg

More Testing

November 2016 (a year into this), we had an appointment with Dr. Rothe when Chad was *not* doing well. This was after the first-degree burn from the wrap applied for "PG."

Chad told Dr. Rothe that he felt like he was in between a bunch of doctors worried about a lawsuit and that his patient care was being neglected. Everyone was worried about "covering their tails" and Chad was falling between the cracks. Everyone the VA contacted ended up saying it was "PG." We were exhausted from all the lies.

After the appointment, Dr. Rothe told me she was really worried about Chad, that she had not seen him like that before. I sent Dr. Rothe an e-mail after I returned home. I told her that I knew in my heart that it was *not* PG, that Chad was sick, and it was much more than anyone thought. I *begged* for more tests to be done.

The next morning, I received a message from Dr. Rothe saying that she received a phone call from the CMO. He asked how Chad was doing, and Dr. Rothe told him that more testing needed to be done. The CMO agreed to pay for more testing. Chad was scheduled for the following tests: ultrasound pelvis, ultrasound abdomen, colonoscopy, TB skin test, allergy blood work, and heavy metal testing. More testing was done, and we started to get answers! This is when we found out the *real reason* why Chad was so sick and why his leg was so bad!

We Finally Have an Answer

In December 2016, thirteen months since the initial "spider bite" ER visit, we *finally* found out what was wrong with Chad. I had asked Dr. Rothe if the MRI with *contrast* could have anything to do with what was going on. I had told everyone that we had seen how Chad's leg did much worse when it was covered and when it got hot. I brought my photo album to all the appointments so the doctors could see the difference in Chad's leg. To date we had seen three sets of ER doctors at the VA, VA Wound Care and Rheumatology, outside Wound Care, Infectious Disease, genetic testing doctor, Wake Forest Dermatology, and Dr. Rothe.

The heavy metal testing revealed that Chad has heavy metal poisoning from the gadolinium, the contrast used in the MRI—he has *gadolinium toxicity*. As a nurse, I had never heard about this before, and neither have any of the other nurses that I have worked with. No one knows about this.

Symptoms associated with gadolinium toxicity/poisoning are as follows, per the Gadolinium Toxicity website and private group:

Short term memory loss, decreased cognitive function, depression, headaches, sleep disorders, chronic fatigue, sinusitis-allergic reactions, muscle spasms and weakness, burning extremities—numbness and tingling, metallic taste, pain in the heart/angina, progressive vision loss, electrifying feeling/vibration within the body.

The website states that "Since at least 1991, it has been known that some Gadolinium would remain in the body of all patients and it could result in a toxic effect. The long-term effects of deposited Gadolinium are still unknown."

The Gadolinium Toxicity website has members from all over the world who have been affected by this toxic heavy metal. They are looking for help and answers. Gadolinium stores in the bones, tissues, and organs. One member in the group had not had an MRI with contrast in nine years and had to have her ovaries removed. She had them test for gadolinium, and it showed up in her biopsy.

The claim was that gadolinium only affected people with kidney issues, but that is not true. Chad's kidneys were perfectly normal. It is also said to be excreted within seventy-two hours after it is administered; that is also not true. Gadolinium is banned in some countries already and is supposed to have a black box warning for use. It is estimated that forty million MRIs are performed yearly in the United States. Chad only had one MRI (while he was admitted to the VA hospital) for suspected osteomyelitis. The contrast (gadolinium) first went to Chad's leg, which was debrided, which is what caused the panniculitis.

Gena Norris

Gena Norris, the wife of Chuck Norris, suffers from gadolinium toxicity as well. She is the one who helped bring this issue into the light. She did interviews in 2017 and 2018, and they were represented by Cutter Law out of California. Gena was extremely sick from multiple MRIs and had to go to China to get treatment (chelation). In the last interview, she said that she was going to be the FDA's worst nightmare. They filed eleven lawsuits against the pharmaceutical companies responsible for this. One of the attorneys for Cutter Law was interviewed and talked about this being a "coverup."

I contacted Cutter Law and was asked to send Chad's test results and medical records showing that he suffered from gadolinium toxicity. Chad was taken on as a client, and we were told that we could not speak about gadolinium toxicity; we were told to be patient and to wait. We were told that it could take years before anything happened.

God Told Us to Tell His Story

Give thanks to the LORD and proclaim his greatness.
Let the whole world know what he has done.
Sing to him; yes, sing his praises.
Tell everyone about his wonderful deeds.

—Psalm 105:1–2

Chad and I were very confused about what to do. Chad was being represented by Cutter Law, and they told us we could not speak about gadolinium toxicity, MRIs, etc. Chad's medical record with the VA does not say anything at all about gadolinium or toxic effects from a heavy metal. We were confused because we knew that God had told us to tell his story. The only reason that Chad is alive with two legs is because God saved him. God gave us a miracle, and we were supposed to tell others about what happened. We started a website to tell what happened but without talking about the MRI and gadolinium toxicity; it was not the whole story.

After much prayer, Chad and I decided that we did not want to continue with Cutter. Not too long after this, Cutter dismissed all cases dealing with gadolinium toxicity. (As of 2020, all gadolinium cases have been dropped. The drug companies are stating that there is no link between gadolinium and adverse side effects.)

Our Mission

As soon as we found out the real reason Chad was so sick, we realized what our mission is in life. We do not want any Veteran to have to go through what we went through. I honestly believe that our nation's Veterans are the least of these. Matthew 25:40 says, "And the King will say, 'I tell you the truth, when you did it to one of these least of these my brothers and sisters, you were doing it to me!" (NLT).

We realized that we want to start a nonprofit farm for Veterans, a refuge away from the VA healthcare system. We want to offer options to help Veterans rehabilitate back into society. We want to offer options besides the standard VA pills and counseling for PTSD. We plan to offer horticulture, art therapy, music therapy, pet therapy in addition to woodworking to help heal our Veterans. These are therapies that we have tried on our own that really work. (I was diagnosed with secondary PTSD during our experience dealing with Chad's sickness and the VA health system.) Chad has started farming and growing our food. He has also taken up playing the drums, and we plan to always have an Old English sheepdog around for therapy.

We prayed for a name for the farm and, of course, God answered. The farm will be named Dayspring Farm. We eventually would like to help our law enforcement men and women in addition to Veterans.

David

Chad and I said that we wanted to help Veterans, that it was our mission in life. In 2019, God gave us an opportunity to "put our money where our mouth is." We had been living in Aurora, Colorado, since September of 2018. (We had been kicked out of the house we were renting in North Carolina, and we decided to move to Colorado to work on our plan for the farm.)

In January 2019 we were contacted by a friend in North Carolina regarding his dad, David, a disabled Vietnam Veteran. David had also recently moved to Colorado from Georgia with his family and was living in Pueblo. We were told that David (who was in a motorized wheelchair) had been living with family and paying all the bills. David's family demanded more money from him, and David said no! David was told on Thursday that if he did not give the family more money, his power would be turned off on Monday.

The family moved out and left David by himself, pretty much helpless. Chad and I were contacted on Thursday about this terrible situation. We prayed about it, and we knew that this was our "Abraham moment." Three days later Chad and I (and two sheepdogs) rented a U-Haul and headed to Pueblo, Colorado, to meet David and to bring him home with us. David's living situation was one of the saddest that I have ever seen.

Chad and I packed up all of David's belongings, and we took him with us back to Aurora. Chad said that he will never forget when we pulled up to David's house in Pueblo, Colorado. David was sitting in his wheelchair in the doorway of his house with the door wide open. David threw his hands in the air, like he had just been rescued from a mission!

David reminded me so much of my dad; it was uncanny. Ironically, David's daughter's name is Naomi. We talked to David about our mission, the farm for Veterans, and he was extremely excited. He said that he knew another Vietnam Veteran who needed help and who could come to the farm.

We discussed putting David on our lease with us and then when it was up, getting a bigger place together. The three of us went to the leasing office to speak with them about our options. David's family did not want us to do this and instead wanted David sent to a homeless shelter in Denver. Chad got into an argument with David's family when we were told to do this. Chad was sticking up for David, but the family ultimately had the last say. Chad and I were upset and heartbroken. David stayed with us for three nights—two disabled Veterans with PTSD, one caregiver, and two Old English sheepdogs in a one-bedroom, eight-hundred-square-foot apartment. One of our sheepdogs, Bernie, would not leave David's side.

As of 2020, David is still in Colorado. He spent six months in a homeless shelter and now has his own apartment and a small dog for a companion.

The Charles George VA

As stated earlier, we had seven meetings at the Charles George VA Hospital with the CMO. Five meetings were with the one CMO, and the last two were with a new CMO. Meeting number 4, the director of the hospital was in attendance as well as the CMO. We were repeatedly asked what we wanted. We always said the same—to figure out what was wrong with Chad and get on with our lives. We told them we did not want to get anyone in trouble; we wanted our medical bills paid and for them to pay for Dr. Rothe. During several of the meetings, I would get so upset I would start shaking; and unfortunately, a couple of the meetings I was so upset that I cried.

On our way to one of the meetings, a van passed us on the interstate going way too fast. A few minutes later the van had wrecked and flipped, and the driver was sitting outside the van on the side of the interstate bleeding. I told Chad that we had to stop even if it made us late for the appointment. I had gloves in the car, and we assisted until EMS arrived. The driver had a large cut on his neck that just missed his carotid artery. I applied pressure to try and stop the bleeding until help arrived.

On our way to another meeting, a disabled Veteran with a cane was stopping people as they turned in to the VA hospital. He stopped us, and we rolled down the window. He told us, "Don't go in there. They will hurt you." We told him unfortunately that we were aware and that we were having a meeting with the CMO about what happened with Chad. He wished us luck and then continued to stop cars as they were turning into the hospital, telling them the same thing.

The VA has taken no accountability for what happened. Chad was blamed; he was called noncompliant and a doctor shopper. During meeting number 7 with the CMO, we were told that we needed to sue them. We told the CMO that we had been turned down by over twenty-five attorneys at that point. He told us that he "wasn't telling us what to do, but if it were him, he would sue." We were told that the VA would not be paying for anything related to gadolinium toxicity, not even the testing for it. As mentioned earlier, Chad's VA medical record does not have his diagnosis of toxic effects of a heavy metal/gadolinium toxicity; it states a diagnosis of ulcer of the lower leg.

Searching for Help

We met with the VSOs (Veteran Service officers) in our county to work on Chad's disability. Before going to the VA hospital, Chad was 70 percent service connected for PTSD. After hearing some of what happened, we were told by two separate VSOs that we needed to get an attorney. One of them gave us the number for an attorney that she thought might be able to help. Everyone that we spoke with about this told us to get an attorney.

Over the course of several years, I reached out to attorney after attorney. I was told repeatedly that we did not have a case because Chad did *not* lose his leg or his life. I tried to explain that the only reason Chad did *not* lose his leg and his life was because I was a nurse and we had to go outside the VA system to get answers. As soon as I mentioned the VA hospital, no one wanted anything to do with us.

We met with an attorney in Charlotte, North Carolina, the first one who agreed to meet with us. As soon as he saw all the files and paperwork I had and heard it was a VA hospital, he said "holy s——" and then told us that he could not take us as clients.

We met with another attorney in Boone, North Carolina, who had represented the wife of a Veteran who had died at the Charles George VA Hospital. (The Veteran was given the incorrect amount of Dilaudid several times and died. Dilaudid is said to be roughly thirty times stronger than morphine. The VA doctor told the wife it was there fault and then later they tried to deny this, taking no accountability for what happened.)

The attorney asked us what kind of money we were talking about. We explained that we weren't interested in money (not what an attorney wants to hear), that we were concerned about future complications from the gadolinium and Chad's VA medical records not showing anything at all about heavy metal poisoning. The attorney told us that we were also looking at a loss of consortium claim since I had to resign from my job to take care of Chad full time. I mentioned that we had paid roughly $1,600 out of pocket for medical supplies (wound care for Chad's leg). The attorney laughed when I said $1,600. He did not want to take us on as clients to go against the VA healthcare system.

The last attorney that we reached out to was when we lived in Colorado in 2019. Our neighbor knew some of the details of our story. She saw an advertisement and suggested we contact him. We thought that this attorney might be different than all the others because in addition to being an attorney, he was also a doctor. I thought, *Finally, this is what we are looking for!*

I e-mailed him directly on Saturday and was shocked to receive an e-mail from him the very next day. He said that he appreciated my detailed e-mail. He asked me if any of the other attorneys that we had reached out to had taken the time to listen to me (as a nurse) and see the medical facts/malpractice behind my concerns. He said that he was not afraid to go against the VA hospital, and he asked several questions about Chad's diagnosis and some of the details of what happened. I e-mailed him back the next day, answering the questions that he asked. I told him about the MRI and the diagnosis of gadolinium toxicity. That was the last time that I heard anything from him.

After this last attorney in Colorado, we realized that it was not meant to be. (We stopped counting at thirty-three attorneys/rejections.) We were reaching out for help, but there is no help for Veterans who are trying to fight the VA health system. We were wanting someone to fight for us, to protect us, to stand up for us. We were looking for help in the wrong place; we were looking for help from the world.

> Lord, you have come to my defense; you have redeemed my life. You have seen the wrong they have done to me, LORD. Be my judge, and prove me right. You have seen the vengeful plots my enemies have laid against me. LORD, you have heard the vile names they call me. You know all about the plans they have made. (Lamentations 3:58–61, NLT)

WLOS

My coworkers reached out to WLOS, the local news station in Asheville, regarding what took place. They came to our house to ask us some questions. They filmed us, but it was not to be aired; this was just to show their bosses the story to see if they wanted to move forward with it. After seeing some of what happened and seeing Chad's leg, they agreed to work on this story.

I communicated with WLOS for months as they contacted Dr. Rothe and the CMO at the VA Hospital. WLOS came to Dr Rothe's office after one of Chad's appointments and did another interview there, this time with Chad and Dr Rothe. This was the interview that was to be aired. The investigative journalist told us that Chad was "red flagged and blacklisted" at the VA hospital.

A couple of weeks before the piece was supposed to air, I was contacted by the reporter. She said that they were going to do the piece on long wait times and not being able to get appointments at the VA hospital (not at all what we reached out to them for). She asked me to get together all of Chad's doctors' appointments with Primary Care, Wound Care, and Rheumatology. The next time I heard from her, she said that the piece would be aired on February 22, 2017, at 11:00 a.m. I told my Hospice friends, and they informed me that the news does not come on at 11:00 a.m.; she must have meant 11:00 p.m.

When the story came on TV, Chad and I were completely shocked! It was all a bunch of lies and garbage. I remember staring at the screen in disbelief. The piece was titled, "Medical Diagnosis Mistakes Impact 12 Million a Year." It stated how the Charles George VA Medical Center had a five-star rating. The piece said that Chad was "waging a war on an infection that six months ago was much larger, blackening the skin." (This was not correct. Chad had multiple infections, but that was not the reason his leg was bad. Also, his leg was black because of the medication (Silvadene) used for the first-degree burn after Wake Forest applied the wrap for "PG.")

Next, the reporter said, "Thomas's medical records showed for months the VA bounced him between VA care and being outsourced to Mission Hospital while the infection spread to the other leg." This was also not correct. The VA denied our referral to Mission Infectious Disease (that is when I contacted the patient advocates), and we went to Mission Hospital on our own.

Then the reporter said, "Thomas's request to the VA for a second opinion was initially denied. And News 13 uncovered that to get a second opinion approved outside the VA. It's the doctor, not the patient, who must agree." (Well, duh! We were denied referrals, and that is why we went outside the VA system for help and answers. The VA doctors told Chad that it was PYODERMA GANGRENOSUM (the primary care doctor wrote that in all caps in Chad's medical record), and Chad was told to follow up with VA Wound Care and Rheumatology.)

The CMO, Dr. Bazemore, stated, "It's the physician who has to generate that consult to go outside. So, to say that the physician has to give permission, well, the physician has to again authorize that care." (Again, no mention of our requests and the VA denials, just more garbage.)

The reporter stated, "Thomas's push for answers got him labeled noncompliant, the VA saying he wasn't following its doctor's orders.

Dr Rothe stated, "He was complying with the orders he was given, but really, the only intervention they were doing at the time was debriding or admitting him to the hospital and putting him on methotrexate, which wasn't really helping him. If Chad and Naomi were listened to really carefully in the beginning, this would have been resolved a lot sooner. That's documented all over his chart— that this is a noncompliant patient, a nonadherent patient."

Dr. Rothe said what isn't documented are the times Thomas's physicians canceled appointments for other emergencies or how long he sat waiting for appointments. Thomas said the wait time "could be hours."

In his interview, Dr Bazemore (CMO) stated, "We have partnerships not only here in the community with Mission and the surrounding areas, but also regionally with Duke, Wake Forest." (This is not correct either. Dr Rothe sent Chad's biopsies to Wake Forest, and we were contacted by WF to attend the physicians' clinical conference. The VA had no partnership with Wake Forest, and the CMO was upset about the biopsies being sent there.)

As stated previously, we reached out to Congressman Mark Meadows about the treatment at the VA hospital. I communicated with his representative for months via e-mail, and she and I spoke often on the phone. WLOS stated:

> We reached out to Congressman Mark Meadows's office about the issue. Here's what they told us when News 13 asked if they've heard complaints about the care the VA in Western North Carolina is providing: "To answer your question: much like you with your reporting, we too have seen firsthand many of the problems with the VA and care of Veterans, particularly with Veterans' benefits. One of the main things our office deals with is streamlining the process of Veterans receiving their proper benefits because there are often such lengthy delays in between when servicemen and women get the benefits they're entitled to… It's probably the top issue we get calls about, from a casework standpoint. It's a significant problem, and yes, we for sure support ideas to reform the process so we can get Veterans' their proper benefits in a much more timely manner. Rep. Meadows feels very strongly about this issue."

There was nothing said about the denied referrals, the misdiagnoses, the negligent treatment, etc.

Dr. Bazemore was interviewed as well as some random doctor that we had never seen before. That doctor expressed the importance of getting a second opinion to prevent misdiagnosis. Again, nothing was said about our repeated denials, about Chad's struggle to get help and answers, about Hospice raising money and finding Dr. Rothe, etc.

When WLOS interviewed the random doctor, this is what was said: "Dr. Mark Graber has worked on similar studies. The next person down the line may not rethink the case, from scratch, you may not rethink the case. If you see them a couple months later and look at the chart and see oh, it's asthma, you don't question that, you just accept that diagnosis."

Graber serves as president of the Society to Improve Diagnosis in Medicine (SIDM). Graber said there are steps doctors can take to catch misdiagnoses. "Things like getting second opinions or taking a time out to consider other possible diagnoses along with other diagnostic tools," Graber said.

I had hundreds of pictures of Chad's leg, from the initial misdiagnosis of the spider bite and I&D in November 2015 until the piece aired in Feb 2017. When the story aired, they showed only three pictures: one was of the Charles George VA Hospital and the other two were pictures of Chad's leg taken during the interview at Dr. Rothe's office. The pictures do not even come close to showing how bad Chad's leg was during this ordeal.

The Mitchell News Journal

I reached out to our local newspaper regarding the treatment at the Charles George VA Hospital. The reporter came out to our house twice to speak with us and to take pictures. He came to one of the appointments that we had with Dr. Rothe and sat in. Chad and I spoke with him, and he also contacted the CMO at the Charles George VA to get their side of the story.

After months and months of communicating with the reporter, I e-mailed him to see how the story was coming. He told me that he was finished with it, but it did not make it into that week's paper. The next week when the story was not in the paper again, I sent him an e-mail. I got an automatic response that he was no longer working with the *Mitchell News Journal*. I called and spoke to his boss, the editor, who told me that the reporter had moved to another state. The editor told me that he had been given our story and that he was working on it. This was in May 2017. In September 2017, the editor e-mailed me a copy of the story the reporter had been working on for me to look over.

The story was titled, "Veteran locked in months-long dispute with VA." The story focused on the VA not paying our medical bills, Dr. Rothe stating she is "never on hold for less than three hours" when calling the VA. The story stated, "The spokeswoman said the VA authorized and paid for two separate second opinions in Chad's case, which is a claim refuted by the Thomases." Of course, this was not true. We went outside the VA for our second opinions when we were denied by the VA, and only after we contacted Senate and Congress did the VA agree to pay for our outside doctors. It is stated in the story that Dr. Rothe said, "VA staff should have done a biopsy when their treatment was not going as expected." She also stated, "I did the biopsy; that's the only way I got the answer."

After reading the story that was e-mailed to me by the *Mitchell News Journal*, I told the editor that we did not want the piece to be in the paper.

Veterans Crisis Hotline

During the five months (November through April) that Chad was being seen at the Charles George VA, Chad's anxiety and PTSD were at an all-time high. He was on prednisone, which makes PTSD much worse, and his anger and rage were out of control. My mom called the Veterans Crisis Hotline twice, and I called them twice as well.

During one of Chad's thirty-minute mental health appointments at the VA (where the provider was fifteen minutes late), she asked Chad how he was doing. Chad told her that he had not been doing well and told her about mom and I calling the Veterans Crisis Line. Chad said the provider's face turned white. She told Chad that there was no record in his chart of anyone calling the Crisis Line and that someone was supposed to contact Mental Health to let them know they needed to check on the Veteran. (That of course did not happen.) One of the times that I reached out to the Crisis Line was when Chad accidentally injured himself, and I did not know what to do.

In my desperate search for help, I contacted the White House. I tried to send a message to President Obama and Mrs. Obama. I received an e-mail from the Veterans Crisis Hotline regarding where I had reached out to Mrs. Obama. The representative said they were going to contact us. A woman from the Veterans Crisis Line called and asked to speak with me first. After she assessed me and made sure that I was not suicidal/homicidal, she asked me if she could speak with Chad.

Chad got on the phone and was telling the representative about our struggle with the VA hospital and some of the details of what we had been through. The representative asked Chad over and over *who* he was targeting and *who* he wanted to kill. Chad told her that he was not targeting anyone and did not want to kill anyone; he just wanted to get some help.

The conversation did not go well, and Chad started having a panic attack. After Chad got off the phone, I called my dad to tell him what happened. Dad then called my uncle who is a retired command sergeant major to tell him about the phone call. After Dad spoke with my uncle, he suggested that we call a local attorney to tell them what happened just in case the Veterans Crisis Line tried to send someone to our house. I called a local attorney that Chad and I knew just to let him know about the phone call as well.

Dr Rothe contacted the Wounded Warrior Project (WWP) about Chad and me, and we were contacted by a representative with them. The WWP was offering a grant that would pay for counseling outside the VA, and Dr. Rothe recommended an excellent counselor that she knew. We were able to see the counselor for a year; Chad and I did all our sessions together. When the grant ran out, we continued seeing the counselor and paid out of pocket for the sessions at a reduced rate that we had agreed upon. The counselor had experience working with Veterans with PTSD, and she was awesome! Her name is Elizabeth Haney, and she wrote a book titled *The Honor was Mine*. Elizabeth counseled Veterans on military bases all over the United States and ended up getting PTSD because of her work dealing with these Veterans.

Chad was 100 percent service connected for PTSD and technically should not have to pay out of pocket for mental health treatment. However, given the choice of getting mental health treatment for free at the VA or paying out of pocket to go outside the VA, we opted to pay out of pocket.

You Planned Evil Against Me

During our struggle to get answers as to why Chad was so sick, we had to fight the VA health system. It is a corrupt and evil system. One of the hospice nurses that I worked with told me several times that our fight reminded her of David and Goliath. In the interview with WLOS, Dr. Rothe said that the VA hospitals should be done away with. Veterans should be given insurance and allowed to pick their primary care doctor. Dr. Rothe stated, "If Chad had continued with their plan, he may have lost his leg and would likely have serious complications of immunosuppression (infection, cancer, or death)."

Chad and I have experienced this evilness firsthand. I would not wish this treatment on my worst enemy. During one of Chad's appointments with Wound Care, a plastic surgeon was debriding his leg. Chad was in intense pain and almost passed out. He remembers being laughed at.

Chad and I have been to four different VA hospitals over the years, and each one was a disaster. In 2014 I worked as a travel nurse at a VA hospital in Salem, Virginia. One night I was given a patient who was in physical restraints because he was considered a danger to himself and others. He was an older patient who was delirious. (Any patient in restraints is a one-on-one patient. He was physically restrained, and then he was given medication to try to calm him down. That is two forms of restraint: chemical and physical.)

I was given this patient in addition to others, and the ER called with an admission to the floor. They tried to give the new patient to me, and I refused. The house supervisor came up to the floor to see what the "problem was," and I explained that I was not leaving my patient by himself, and they could fire me if they wanted to. The doctor came to see the patient, and I suggested a medication that I had given in the ER with positive results. The doctor stated that the medication I mentioned was known to have adverse effects on elderly patients, I explained that everything they had tried was not ⟨…⟩ and it was worth giving it a shot.

He agreed to try the medication I suggested and later came back to the floor to see that the patient had calmed down significantly since the new medication was given. (In the news in August 2020 was a Louisville VA hospital who let a neighbor illegally decide a Veteran's fate. In the article it states that the Veteran went to the VA hospital in 2019 for back pain and died several weeks later. He went in for back pain, he was restrained seventeen times, he was admitted involuntarily and was sent to a locked mental unit twice. Before going to the hospital, the Veteran lived at home by himself, he handled his own finances, and he had a service dog. Once the Veteran went to the VA for help, he was diagnosed with dementia, delirium, and schizophrenia, among others.)

One night I went into work at the VA in Virginia, and there was a lot of commotion. A patient, who was a Vietnam Veteran, was curled up in a ball in the fetal position under the sink in his room, having a panic attack. I asked what was going on and was told that he was assigned an Asian nurse, and when he saw her, he must have had a flashback. Everyone was crowded around him, and several people were up in his face. I was furious. I told them to leave him alone and to give him some space. (You do not get in someone's face who is having a panic attack.)

Later that night, I was charting at the nurse's station, and the Veteran came out to talk. He apologized for what happened earlier, and he was embarrassed. I told him that he did not have anything to apologize for, that we were the ones who should apologize to him.

The late John Lewis said, "If you see something that is not right, not fair, not just, you have a moral obligation to do something about it." We have seen firsthand how our nation's Veterans are treated. We have seen firsthand how hard it is to fight for what is right. We have seen how hard it is to reach out for help. I had to speak for Chad when he was unable to speak for himself. I had to stand up for my Veteran and refuse to take no for answer.

Genesis 50:20 says, "You intended to harm me, but God intended it all for good. He brought me to this position so I could save the lives of many people" (NLT).

The men and women who serve our country deserve better than this. As a nurse, I know that mistakes happen all the time. While what happened to us may have started as a mistake, what followed was unethical, unlawful, corrupt, and just plain mean.

Chad and I know that we are not alone in our experience dealing with the Veterans administration system. This is not a one-time, isolated event. According to one article, in 2018 $6.2 million was budgeted for suicide prevention outreach for our Veterans. Out of that, only $57,000 was spent (which is less than 1 percent.)

In April 2019, two Veterans committed suicide at two separate VA hospitals in Georgia. In August 2019, a former VA doctor (pathologist) was charged with three counts of involuntary manslaughter. The article from CNN states the doctor "entered false and misleading diagnoses into the medical records of patients in his care, contributing to the death of three of them, according to a criminal indictment. In one case, the indictment says, a patient died of prostate cancer after Levy had concluded that test results showed the patient did not have cancer." In August 2019, a Veteran committed suicide in the parking lot at the Charles George VA Hospital in Asheville, North Carolina. In the news in July 2020 was the death of seven elderly Veterans who were given insulin when they were either not diabetic or did not need the insulin at all. The staff member plead guilty to seven counts of second-degree murder.

He Gives and Takes Away

Since opening my heart to Jesus in 2016, Chad and I have seen a lot of heartache. In addition to Chad's sickness and our struggle to find answers, we have lost three out of our four Old English sheepdogs, who were our children.

We have lost two grandmothers, we lost my dad, and we lost Chad's best friend to suicide (he shot himself in the heart). I totaled Chad's car, I resigned to take care of Chad full time and went from making three thousand dollars a month to five hundred dollars as a VA caregiver. We were kicked out of a house we were renting for being "hillbillies," for parking the wrong way in the driveway (horizontally versus vertically), for weeds in the gravel driveway, and for bird poop on the deck. We were told to "Get Out Now!" via e-mail. We were given our security deposit back, and then nine months after we moved out, we were accused of stealing. (I know that God has a good sense of humor.)

But even with all this sadness, God has brought us blessing after blessing! Job 1:21 says, "I came naked from my mother's womb, and I will be naked when I leave. The Lord gave me what I had, and the Lord has taken it away. Praise the name of the Lord!" (NLT)

Daddy

Timothy James Howard was a great guy. He had his issues, as we all do, but he had a great heart. He and my mom built a company from the ground up. Dad was gone away a lot on business and worked extremely hard to make this dream of theirs come true. When Arundel and I were in middle school, we took a family vacation to see our grandparents in Canada. This was one of the few trips that dad was able to go with us. While we were away, Dad's business partner emptied their bank account and took everything that we had. Dad never recovered from this, and then he started drinking. Our lives were never the same again.

Dad was kind. He was funny. He was a great dad. He called us the "crying Howards" and said that I, of course, was the worst one. (One hospice patient told me that he had nine children, and he had never seen anyone cry as much as I did.) After opening my heart to Jesus, I met daddy one day and told him that I was thirty-six years old and that I finally believed in God. He hung his head and cried. He said it was his fault. Our family did not grow up knowing who God was, but we did have something that a lot of other families did not have, and that was love.

Daddy suffered from COPD and had been on oxygen for years. I recommended that he reach out to Hospice because they also provided palliative care. I did not know how poor his health was and was shocked when he was admitted to Hospice with stage-3 COPD. To qualify for Hospice, the doctor must believe that the patient has six months or less to live.

In October 2016 dad was admitted to the hospital, and we were told that he could not go back home where he had been living with his girlfriend. The doctor knew dad's home situation and knew that dad was on a pain pump. Chad, Arundel, and I discussed what to do, and we decided that we were going to take care of dad. We did not know how long he had, but we did not want him to go into a nursing home (Dad's worst fear), and he could not go back to where he had been living. Daddy could not believe that Arundel and I were going to take care of him. As we were leaving the hospital, he asked me if we were sure about it, and I told him of course we were! I had posted on Facebook where we needed to find a place to rent ASAP, and the next day someone reached out to me.

Arundel and I took care of daddy for the last month of his life. We rented a house, and Arundel stayed with him 24/7. I had my hands full with Chad, the VA, Wake Forest, Dr. Rothe, etc., but tried to go over and help as much as I could. I would pick up food and bring it over, and we would all hang out. Dad apologized to me for being a bad father, and I apologized for being a bad daughter. When I could, I would stay up and watch daddy sleep so Arundel could get some rest. Dad had a bad habit of pulling his oxygen off in his sleep, and his oxygen level would drop very quickly. Daddy was so happy for us all to be together again; he asked when he was going to wake up from the dream.

This was Daddy's note to Arundel when he was in the hospital:

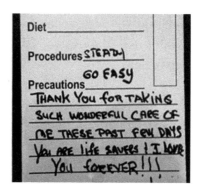

In November dad started declining rapidly and was having terminal agitation (restlessness, sleeplessness, anxiety). One of the hospice nurses saw in a report where dad was having issues sleeping and remembered that he grew up Catholic. She asked me if dad would want a Catholic priest to come and talk to him. We asked dad, and he said yes. On Friday, November 4, 2016, daddy asked Jesus for forgiveness of his sins. Two days later he died.

Arundel and I are so thankful that we were able to take care of daddy his last month of life. It was one of the hardest things that we have ever had to do, but what an honor it was to take care of dad and for him to know how loved he was! (When Arundel and I were little, our family went tubing down the river, and Arundel got stuck under a rock. Daddy jumped in and saved her. In the end, Arundel helped save Daddy's life, and he was so grateful for what she did for him!)

Daddy's life could have ended a lot differently, and I thank God for his grace and mercy. (Mom and Dad were married for almost twenty-five years and got divorced after Arundel and I graduated high school.) Mom was able to come see daddy; they forgave each other and were able to say goodbye. It was an incredibly special and sad moment in our lives.

Arundel and I took daddy's ashes with us to Colorado and spread some of them at Garden of the Gods. We played Aaron Neville's "Amazing Grace," and we thanked God for the best dad he could have possibly given us.

Chad

On Sunday, July 9, 2017, Chad rededicated his life to Christ! We went to church with his mom and stepdad that morning, and it seemed like the whole sermon was meant for us. We had a rough morning dealing with Chad's PTSD, and I remember praying for him on the way to church. For once I did not know what to say, and I kept my mouth shut (rarely does that happen).

The verse on the flyer that day was Matthew 11:28: "Then Jesus said, 'Come to me, all of you who are weary and carry heavy burdens, and I will give you rest'" (NLT). Chad's stepdad sang a beautiful song and played his guitar. The pastor told everyone that they were baptizing people that day (we did not know this was happening), and he asked if anyone else wanted to be baptized. Chad jumped up without hesitation and immediately walked up to the front of the church. Chad was baptized in long pants and a long-sleeve shirt. He was so excited; he did not care. Chad's mom and I were both so shocked and excited. We both had tears streaming down our faces.

It's Just Too Much

November 1, 2017, will be a day that I will never forget. Chad and I had a mental health appointment in Asheville with Elizabeth Haney. After the appointment, we headed to Dr. Rothe's office in Burnsville to see her PA. Chad had been bitten by a deer tick the night before and had an immediate local reaction. Dr. Rothe wanted Chad to see the PA to determine if antibiotics needed to be started for Lyme disease. I dropped Chad off at the office and had to go home to get the tick so it could be sent off for analysis.

It was about a half an hour drive each way, and I called Arundel, overwhelmed and crying. I told Arundel, "It's just too much!" Arundel posted a message on Facebook, asking for prayers for Chad and me.

After the appointment, Chad and I headed to the pharmacy to pick up his antibiotic to try to prevent Lyme disease from the tick bite. Arundel called my cell phone as we were almost to the pharmacy. She asked me if Chad was in the car with me, and I told her that he was. She told me that several people from the police and sheriff's department had been trying to get in touch with us, and they contacted her. Arundel told me that Chris, Chad's best friend, had just committed suicide. Chad said that my face turned white, and he took the phone out of my hand and continued to speak to Arundel. We later learned that Chris had shot himself in the heart, in front of some of his coworkers. I learned that day that I will never say that anything is "just too much."

Nana Josephine

In December 2017, Chad and I moved to Wolf Laurel in Mars Hill, North Carolina. We moved closer to my grandmother (my mom's mother) so that I could help take care of her. My aunt was Nana's full-time caregiver, and she needed some help. My uncles paid me six hundred dollars a month to help with Nana; that was more money than I made as Chad's VA caregiver. I took Nana to all her doctor's appointments and helped her with her bills and groceries.

We did not grow up around Nana and Grandpa, and this was such an awesome experience getting to spend time with her. She told me all kinds of hilarious stories about her and grandpa and their eight children. I looked forward to spending time with her, and she felt the same way about me. She made me laugh so hard. She was a wonderfully amazing woman. She had one eye (cataract surgery gone wrong), one boob (breast cancer), and had a pig valve in her heart. She told people to call her "lucky." She said it could always be worse; she could have no eyes and no boobs.

One day, on the way to Nana's cardiology appointment, Nana and I were talking about the passing of Billy Graham. She told me that she and Grandpa had seen Billy Graham in Boston when they were younger. She said if Billy Graham did not get into heaven, then there was not any hope for the rest of us. Nana asked me if there was a secret to getting into heaven. This was my opportunity to tell her about Jesus and blew it! I remember telling our pastor at the time about it, and I was so upset. When I got home that day, I found out that Billy's wife's maiden name was Bell; she was Ruth Bell. *Ruth* is my middle name and *Bell* was Nana's last name. I called Nana and told her about it and told her that was her and I, Ruth Bell.

I watched Nana decline over the nine months that I helped take care of her. She went from being able to walk with a walker to me pushing her in a wheelchair. I told my mom about Nana's decline and that she was not doing well. I took Nana to an appointment one day to get her labs drawn with her primary care doctor, and her oxygen was low. They ended up admitting her into the hospital, putting her on oxygen and telling her that she was in heart failure. She was sent home days later with a consult to Hospice.

Nana feared Hospice as a lot of people do, so I explained things to her. I explained why Hospice uses morphine and that she did not have to be afraid of anything. I reassured her that they would treat her like family. I recommended the hospice that Arundel and I worked for, the same hospice that took care of daddy. I told her that they would take excellent care of her, and there was nothing for her to worry about. One night I stayed until after midnight with Nana, and I asked her if I could read a prayer to her before she went to bed. I read her a salvation prayer, and she said that she loved it; she said it was beautiful.

One Sunday, as Chad and I were getting ready for church, Nana's hospice nurse called me. She said she was not exactly sure what was going on. Nana had a stroke early that morning, and she was not sure if she was starting the dying process. Chad and I headed to see Nana, and we stopped at church so we could speak to the pastor. The pastor knew that I thought I had blown my opportunity to speak to Nana about Jesus, and he said a prayer for us all.

When Nana woke up that day and saw me, she asked me to say a prayer for her. That was not something Nana would normally ask for. I told Chad that *this* was our opportunity, and I was going to do it that day! I drove Chad and the sheepdogs back to the house, and I went back to spend time with Nana. I said Joshua 1:9 over and over on my way back to her apartment. Joshua 1:9: "This is my command—be strong and courageous! Do not be afraid or discouraged. For the LORD your God is with you wherever you go" (NLT). Nana was sleeping for a good while, and then not long after Arundel arrived, she woke up. Arundel and I knew that this was it; God placed us here for a reason at that time.

We closed the door so we could talk to Nana. I explained to Nana that the prayer I read to her that night was a salvation prayer. We explained to her what that meant and asked her if she wanted us to read it to her, and she could repeat it. She said yes! It was one of the sweetest things that I have ever heard in my life. Nana, with her new slurred speech from the stroke, repeated the prayer back as I read it to her. Our eighty-eight-year-old grandmother asked Jesus for forgiveness of her sins that day! Chad asked Nana later if she understood the importance of what happened and told her that she now had a "seat at the table." Nana, being the goober that she was, said, "Well I hope so because I am a great cook!" Revelation 3:20: "Look! I stand at the door and knock. If you hear my voice and open the door, I will come in, and we will share a meal together as friends" (NLT).

Four days later, Nana passed away. Nana was surrounded by her family, and she knew how much she was loved. I am forever grateful to God for such an amazing opportunity to help take care of Nana during her last months on this earth.

A Second Chance

After all the things I have done in my life, I deserve death, prison, punishment. I do not deserve to be happy, and I certainly do not deserve a second chance.

When Jesus came into my heart, I felt like I had been asleep my whole life. I felt like someone had turned a light on inside of me. I had been living in darkness, and God showed me the light. I was defeated, I was exhausted, and I was hopeless. I was 190 pounds (I am roughly five feet two inches); I weighed the same as what Chad weighed in Basic Training. I suffered from eating disorders, spending seven years as a bulimic.

I cared what the world thought and everyone in it thought. Before making a decision, I asked others, "What do you think I should do?" I was a people pleaser. I did not want to disappoint anyone; I did not want to let anyone down. I did not want to ask for help, and I did not want to give up control.

I know that we all have a purpose in this life, a reason for being here. I know that if God had not allowed me to be a nurse, Chad would not be alive today. Chad is alive for a reason. No one can take credit for what happened but God! Ephesians 2:4–5 says, "But God is so rich in mercy, and he loved us so much, that even though we were dead because of our sins, he gave us life when he raised Christ from the dead (NLT). It is only by God's grace that you have been saved!

Chad and I were brokenhearted after losing three of our four Old English sheepdogs. Like I said earlier, they were our children. We had Chet Bella Weenie for almost thirteen years; we got him when he was eight weeks old. But God, being the Amazing Father that he is, had something wonderful in store for us, something that we would never have dreamed of. In February 2020, after almost sixteen years of marriage (at the age of forty and forty-three years old) Chad and I were blessed with a beautiful baby girl. Her name is

Abigail Faith Thomas, and she was born on my mother's birthday. In Hebrew *Abigail* means "the father's joy/gives joy."

God has given us an opportunity to help other Veterans, to be a voice for those who cannot speak for themselves. We will have a farm for Veterans someday. It is up to God when and where, but we know that it will happen. We look forward to taking care of those men and women who have served this great country.

God has changed everything about our lives. Chad and I are not the same people that we used to be, and I am forever grateful for that. God has given us a miracle. *He* has given us hope. *He* has given us peace. *He* has given us joy. *He* has made us children again.

> I tell you the truth, unless you turn from your sins and become like little children, you will never get into the Kingdom of Heaven. So anyone who becomes as humble as this little child is the greatest in the Kingdom of Heaven. (Matthew 18:3–4, NLT).

References

Emert, Jennifer. 2017, February 22. "Medical diagnosis mistakes impact 12 million a year." https://wlos.com/news/news-13-investigates/diagnosis-mistakes-12-million-happen-a-year

Full Measure Staff. 2017, June 11. "MRI Changes. Fighting for her Life." http://fullmeasure.news/news/cover-story/mri-06-11-2017

Full Measure Staff. 2018, August 12. "MRI Changes. Fighting for her Life." http://fullmeasure.news/news/cover-story/mri-changes-08-07-2018

Gadolinium Toxicity. "Shedding light on the effects of retained gadolinium from Contrast MRI." https://gadoliniumtoxicity.com/

Holcombe, Madeline. 2019, August 21. "Former VA doctor is charged with involuntary manslaughter in the death of 3 patients." *CNN.* https://www.cnn.com/2019/08/21/us/va-doctor-involuntary-manslaughter-intoxication/index.html

Ladd, Sarah. 2020, August 19. "Louisville VA hospital let neighbor illegally decide veteran's fate, report says." https://www.courier-journal.com/story/news/local/2020/08/19/inspector-general-louisville-va-center-violated-patients-rights/3300483001/

Mark, Michelle. 2020, July 16. "A West Virginia nursing assistant admitted to intentionally killing 7 patients with fatal doses of insulin." https://www.insider.com/west-virginia-nursing-assistant-admits-to-killing-7-patients-2020-7

Rhine Law Firm P.C. 2017, October 17. "NC Hospital Held Responsible for Veteran's Death." https://www.carolinaaccidentattorneys.com/blog/2017/october/nc-hospital-held-responsible-for-veteran-s-death/

Wentling, Nikki. 2018, December 17. "VA leaves nearly $5 million unused in 2018 campaign to battle suicide, watchdog finds." *Stars and Stripes.* https://www.stripes.com/news/va-leaves-nearly-5-million-unused-in-2018-campaign-to-battle-suicide-watchdog-finds-1.561146

About the Author

Naomi Ruth Thomas is originally from Hartford, Connecticut. She has lived in ten different states but has spent the majority of her life in the mountains of North Carolina. Naomi is an identical twin. Their mother did not know she was having twins until they were born, and Naomi was a "surprise."

Naomi has worked in many different career fields ranging from cook, waitress, lifeguard, bartender, gas station attendant, cash office clerk, plywood salesman, Starbucks barista, and massage therapist. Naomi went back to school when she was thirty years old to become a nurse. She got her RN/ADN in 2012 and her BSN in 2014. Naomi worked as a nurse for four years before resigning as a hospice nurse to take care of her Veteran husband Chad full time. Naomi married her high school sweetheart, and after almost sixteen years of marriage, they were blessed with a beautiful baby girl. They named her Abigail Faith Thomas.

Although she grew up in the "Bible Belt," Naomi did not grow up believing in God. She thought that people who did believe in God were crazy. Then in 2016, after a life-altering experience, Naomi accepted Jesus into her heart. Naomi is now a faithful follower of Jesus and is so grateful for a second chance.

Naomi enjoys spending time with her family. She loves animals (especially dogs) and enjoys bird watching. She and her husband plan to start a 501(c) Farm for Veterans.

CPSIA information can be obtained
at www.ICGtesting.com
Printed in the USA
BVHW020303300922
648347BV00003BA/55